Maria
The Story of my Life

Maria Taddei

© Maria Taddei, 2018

Epilogue ©
Silvano Taddei, 2019

All Rights Reserved

Revised Second Edition

ISBN: 9781070409535

Contents

1.	Visiting my Roots	1
2.	Portadown	21
3.	On Pilgrimage	39
4.	Socialising	43
5.	Tying the Knot	53
6.	Early Days	67
7.	Changes	75
8.	Family Life	81
9.	More Changes	87
10.	Moving to Kerry	93
11.	Life Goes On	105
12.	Epilogue	113

Dedicated to my parents Rocco and Lidia,
my loving husband Silvano,
and to my beautiful children
and grandchildren

Life is a journey...

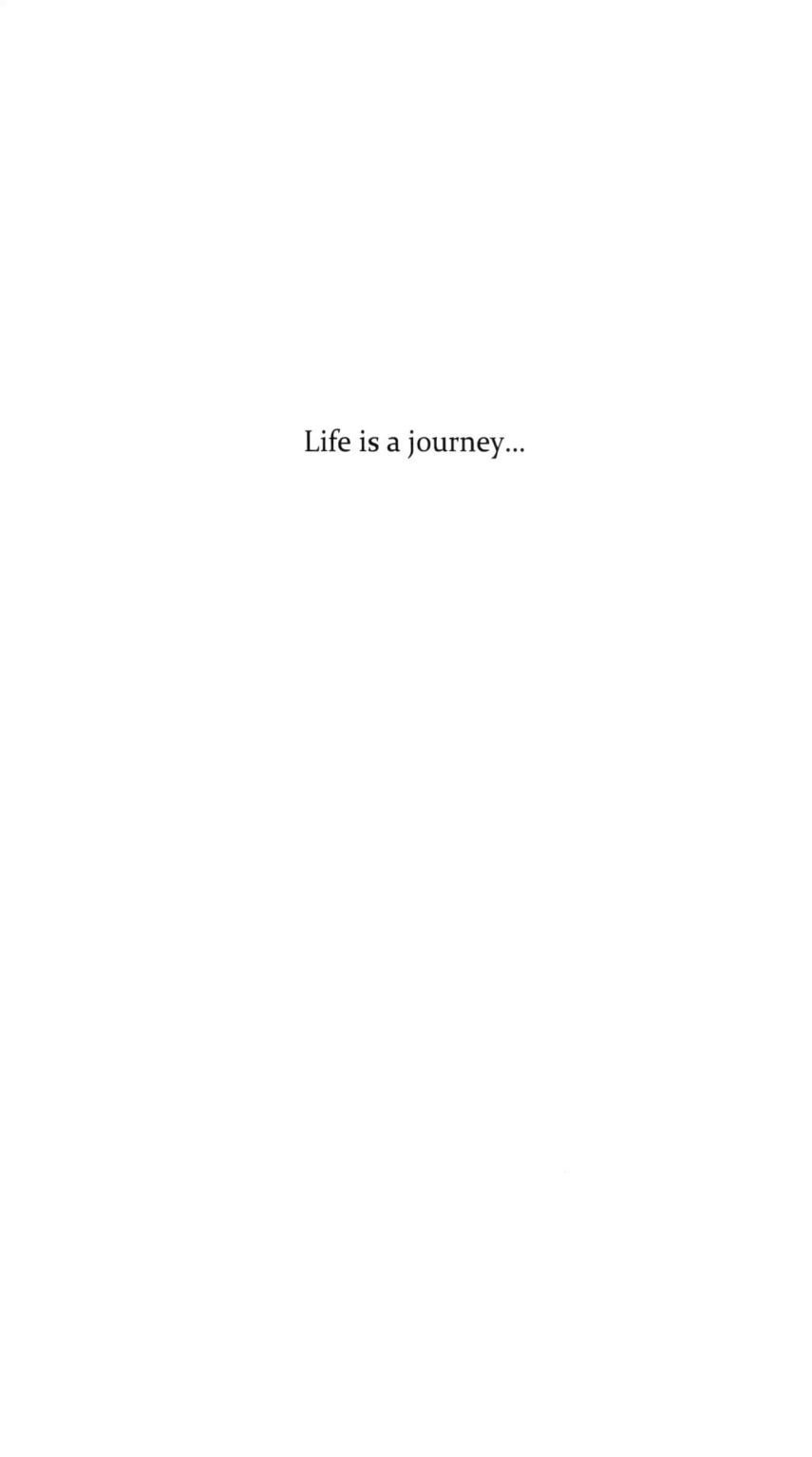

Chapter One

- Visiting my Roots -

I was nine years old the first time I saw my mother's birth place. We had been travelling for three days and the journey was gruelling. My mother was both excited and apprehensive at seeing her homeland and family after eleven years. The Second World War had ended and the borders were open for the first time. It was about six in the evening when we arrived, and very dark as there was no lighting on the road. What is more, I was to learn when we arrived at the house that there was no electricity there either. Everything looked eerie to me and the noises were strange – unfamiliar. A large door opened and a woman stood there with a candle in her hand; the light from same casting flickering shadows on her face. I was scared. So was my older brother Mario, who hid behind my mother's skirt.

This was our first introduction to our father's sister. Her name was Emilia. She was a small woman who talked ninety to the dozen, had never married and had remained in the family home. Unlike the rest of her siblings, she had freckled skin and, to my astonishment, red hair!

She worked very hard, my aunt. She kept chickens, a pig, grew her own vegetables, and made her own bleach, soap and candles. She knew a lot about herbs and, as doctors were hard to reach in the area, she made infusions of these to treat both herself and others in the village for any minor illness. She was, you could say, very self-sufficient, her homestead providing all her needs.

She greeted us and ushered us into the house. I looked around the kitchen. There was a huge open fire with logs burning brightly and a big cauldron-like pot bubbling merrily away, suspended from an iron bracket somewhere in the fireplace. This was where all the meals were cooked. There was very little furniture; a table and four chairs, and a small dresser where the crockery was kept. The sink had no taps and I wondered at that. Then I learned there was no running water. All the water for the house was drawn from a well that stood outside the door. We were tired from the long journey so we climbed the stone stairs to the bedroom that was to be ours for the duration of our stay. There were two huge beds in the room, with iron bedsteads, and they were higher than the beds we had at home so I climbed in, wishing I was back in Ireland; but I soon fell asleep from sheer exhaustion.

I awoke to the sound of a donkey braying loudly and chickens squawking in competition with each other as to who could make the loudest noise. I sat up and took stock of my surroundings. My mother was already up and washing at a stand that held a china basin and a jug of water. Bright sunshine flooded the room, and for a moment I was puzzled, trying to get my bearings. Then I remembered I was in Italy, in the very place my mother had told me about ever since I could remember. This was her home! I jumped out of bed and made for the window, anxious to get my first glimpse of the place in the daylight. The sun shone brilliantly and it cheered me up no end, after the gloom and shadows of the night before. A pretty valley stretched out before me. I could see rows and rows of vines, some trees, a river and a few houses in the distance, and beautiful mountains all around. I splashed some water on my face, got hurriedly dressed, and made my way downstairs to the kitchen. Breakfast was delicious; homemade bread and a bowl of warm milk that had a dash of coffee and sugar in it. We rushed our meal as we were anxious to go outside and explore our surroundings and meet my mother's people. Our house was the first house, on the edge of the village.

* * *

The village of Casalattico, better known as 'Casale' to the locals, rests on a hillock in the Valle Di Comino on the lower slopes of the

Abruzzi mountains. Fourteen hundred feet above sea level, a rural and pastoral area, it is also known as the *Valley of the Emigrants*. It is surrounded by a number of hamlets, the highest of which is Montattico, at twenty-four hundred feet. Due to severe poverty and hardship, families were forced to seek their living far from their native land. Many went to France, America, England, Scotland, and in the case of my own family, Ireland. My father, Rocco Cafolla, born in 1897, was the youngest of six children. Rosa, the eldest sister, had married Carmine Magliocco, a young man whose family had, many years before, emigrated to Scotland. He returned to his father's village to find a wife, fell in love with Rosa, married her and brought her back to Scotland. From there they went to Portadown, Northern Ireland and set up a business. They had seven children. Angelo, the eldest brother, joined them there later. He married Lucia Taddei and they had six children. Mario, another brother, was learning to be a tailor, but contracted tuberculosis (TB) and died at the young age of twenty-four. Teodora married a man from Rome called Ottorino Raimondi. He had been widowed and had a young son, who later became a priest and went to the missions. They had a son call Franco and settled in Rome. My father left in 1917 to work with his brother-in-law in Ireland. He was small in stature with black wavy hair and brown eyes – a quiet, patient, witty man.

Lidia Cassoni, my mother, was the youngest of three children. Anastasia, the eldest girl, was small and petite, and very ladylike. Nicolino, the only boy, was tall and slim, gentle and patient. Lidia was tall, well built, and a bit of a tomboy, full of life – a lady, but not ladylike. Their father, Amedeo, was a well-educated gentleman, portly in stature, with dark hair and eyes, and a luxurious moustache. He wore fine clothes and sported a pocket watch suspended from a gold chain. He had a good position in the bank and had a small grocery shop in the centre of the village. His wife, Marianina Fusciardi, was a local girl, one of seven sisters, and the family were comfortably off.

* * *

When my mother was five years old, tragedy struck. Her mother, my grandmother, died during the birth of her fourth child, a little girl who died with her. My grandfather was devastated. Although he was only thirty-five at the time, he never married again. The children were reared by aunts. Later on, the girls went to boarding school in Sora, a large town about forty miles from the village, and Nicolino went on to college. For a few years, Anastasia looked after the grocery shop, and Lidia preferred looking after the house. To be fair, their father wanted them to take turns, but the two girls decided to stay in their places of preference. They had a happy life, and their father would often hold little parties in the house, at various 'festas' or feast days. And they would dance.

Anastasia married her childhood sweetheart, Angelo Morelli, a young man who had emigrated to Ireland, in 1916, and they had three sons; Nino, Corrado and Guido. They settled in Portstewart, a seaside resort in Northern Ireland. Nicolino was engaged to a young girl from Sora, but she died at the age of twenty-one from TB. Amedeo started a type of credit union in the village, but unfortunately it went bust and he lost everything, which resulted in him and my mother having to leave the village and try and start over in Ireland. Nicolino stayed to complete his education. When the war started he was conscripted into the Italian army and found himself in India, where he was taken prisoner and spent five years in a concentration camp. After the war, in the early 1950's, he met a young woman in Sora called Lina Greco. They married and, due to circumstances, they also emigrated to Ireland. They stayed with us until after the birth of their first daughter, Anna Maria, and then moved to Coleraine where Uncle Angelo Morelli let them a shop. They had another daughter, Marisa, four years later. But the fish and chip business didn't suit Nicolino, so they moved to London, where an old friend of their youth from Casalattico, Charles Forte, later to become Lord Forte, gave him a job as his accountant, which was his profession. He worked there in the Café Royale offices in Piccadilly Circus until his retirement. Anna Maria became an oncologist, and Marisa a financial advisor.

Amedeo and Lidia settled in Cork city, where a relative rented them a fish and chip shop. For my grandfather, this was an awful hardship. Learning this trade was very difficult for him. The fish and chips were cooked in pans that were fuelled by coal, and the dripping that was used was smelly and greasy. Extractors were non-existent, so the smell was hard to get rid of. Lidia was twenty years old and neither of them spoke English. They found the damp weather hard to contend with. Also, Cork was a long way from Portstewart, where Anastasia was. It took two days to make the journey in the old, slow coal-fuelled trains. They stayed in Cork for nine years. During a stay with her sister, Lidia met up with my father. He was almost forty years old, ten years her senior. They got married in Portstewart on 1st February, 1937 and settled in Portadown. My brother was born on 8th November the same year.

I followed in November of 1939 – the year the Second World War started. My mother would laughingly say I started it with the racket I put up at my birth. In 1940, after Italy's declaration of war, my father was arrested as a hostile alien, even though he had been in Ireland since he was a young lad of seventeen. But as he still held an Italian passport he was held overnight in Crumlin

Road Jail and then shipped to the Isle of Man for internment in a concentration camp, where he was to stay for five years, along with many others, one of whom was his brother-in-law. Some men were put on the ship, the *Arandora Star*, which was torpedoed en route to Canada. Hundreds died that day. My mother suffered great hardship during this period. She was a British citizen as she was born in Derry during a visit by her mother to relatives. Because of this, she was free to come and go, but her sister and cousin, who still held Italian nationality, were placed under house arrest. Thankfully, the authorities allowed her and her son to stay with us. They were often harassed by hostile people of the town, and always in a state of anxiety for their husbands, having no contact for several months and not knowing where they were sent. It was five years before they, and many others, were to see their loved ones again.

* * *

Meanwhile, back in Italy, this quiet little village of Casale became part of the Gustav line, one of the fronts during the war, for the Battle of Cassino. High on a mountain-top above Cassino was a Benedictine monastery called Montecassino. It was difficult to capture because of its position. It was one of the hardest battles of the war, and resulted in thousands of deaths.

As the crow flies, the highest point—Montattico—situated above Casalattico, was very near to Montecassino, so they mounted heavy guns up there. My mother and her sister were out of their minds with worry, as my aunt had sent her two young sons a few months previously to stay with their paternal grandmother there for a holiday. For six years they had no word of them, didn't know if they were dead or alive, or if indeed they had any family left. There was absolutely no communication with their village, and the only information they had as to how the war was progressing was via the BBC broadcasts on the radio, or the Movietone News at the cinema. They would often liken this time in their lives to living in hell. I often thought how strong and brave these women were and, when I would comment on this years later, when I realised just what they did go through, they would say, "It was faith and prayer that sustained us during those dark years."

* * *

In 1945, my dad came home. I remember being very shy towards whom to me was a stranger. He was very pale and thin, but there was great rejoicing in our home that day. It was a year later that our young cousins and their grandmother were found. They had at first been in an asylum somewhere in Naples, and then in a displaced persons camp; and it was by sheer chance – but surely it was the answer to years of devout prayer – that the commander of the camp was from Portstewart, their hometown. He recognised the name on the camp list and he sent for them and asked them their father's name. A short time later they were flown home in an RAF plane. We were all at the military airport to meet them. Their brother, who had lived with us during the years we were all separated, was meeting his brothers for what he said was the first time; as he was the youngest and was only five years old when they left. Two very thin boys got out of the plane. The oldest was now fourteen years old and weighed only six stone. The other was twelve and very undernourished. I was seven years old at the time but I will always remember the emotions of that meeting; such joy, tinged with such sorrow for all the missing years of their childhood. God had been good to us. He brought everyone back safely. By now, my mother was receiving letters from her village. The people had slowly returned to what was left of their homes and belongings, which was basically nothing. What furnishings they had was used for firewood by the soldiers that had infiltrated their homes. Everything was either taken or destroyed. The houses were full of lice and fleas; and hand grenades, bullets, guns and mines littered the area. No-one had any bed linen and all had very few household goods. Malaria was rife, malnutrition too, and hunger. A lot of men from the area who had taken to hiding in the higher mountains were either killed or sent to labour camps in Austria and Germany. Many never returned. The war had ended, but now the war for survival had begun. My mother sent back parcels of clothes, tea, chocolate, money, as did many others who were abroad; but the birth of my baby sister Rina in 1947 was to delay her return to Italy for another year.

* * *

The mountain road was rough and we kicked at the stones as we made our way to the piazza. Our progress was slow as people stopped us every few yards to talk to my mother. They hugged and kissed and pinched our cheeks, and each one was relating the horrors that had befallen them since they had last seen each other. I looked in amazement at the scene around us. The women were dressed in long black dresses with big black aprons around their waists, and some kind of white scarf on their heads. Some of them were carrying big, clay jug-like pots with spouts. Others had bundles of sticks. One young girl of about ten years old had a big wicker basket full of clothes – all balanced on their heads! This was the normal way of carrying things, so that hands were always left free to do other things, or tend to babies. They made it look so easy that my brother and I had to have a go. We couldn't even lift the pots on to our heads, let alone carry them. The young girl was on her way to the river to wash the clothes. Later on, we became friends. Her name was Eleonora, and it was a friendship that was to last many years.

The houses were all made of stone work with red roofs, and they lined either side of a narrow road, to the left and right of the square. The little church dominated most of the space, its bell tower rising proudly above the rooftops. As we made our way up the long, narrow street, a little old lady came hurrying towards us crying and pumping her arms up and down. This was my first encounter with my great-grandmother. How she ever survived the trauma of events at such an age I will never know. She was so frail looking, but her embrace was fierce and strong and she smothered us with kisses and hugs, crying '*Lidia, Lidia*' with every kiss. My brother and I soon got fed up with all the aunts and relatives that seemed to come out of every corner of the woodwork. I never knew we had that much family, and, like children do, we made our escape. At that moment, we heard the sound of other children and followed the noise. To our surprise there was a school at the top of the street, and we could see children in a small, fenced-in playground, supervised by two nuns. The children were all wearing smocks; the girls in bright blue and the boys in navy with white collars. We started to giggle because the boys looked funny to us with their smocks over their trousers. My brother thought they were a bunch of sissies. This type of uniform was designed so that all children, rich or poor, looked the same. For ten minutes or so we stared at them and they stared at us. We must have stood out like sore thumbs, with our socks and shoes and fine clothes. Most of the children were barefooted. Some of them were bowlegged with rickets due to malnutrition, and all were as brown as berries and thin as rakes. The two nuns waved us to go over, but like the good brave children we were, we turned on our heels and ran back to the house. Although we understood the language well, we had some difficulty speaking it, hence our reluctance to approach the nuns.

Dinner was ready so we returned to the house, after which everybody went to sleep, a 'siesta' they called it. This was new to us. Back home, nobody went to sleep in the afternoon unless they were ill. We had to conform, but I read a few comics I had brought with me instead. I couldn't sleep even if I tried. I was looking forward to going to the next village which was a mile from this one, but I could see it from the upstairs window. It was called *San Andrea*. There didn't seem to be any cars anywhere. People walked or rode on donkeys. Neither did there seem to be any kind of machinery of any description. I could see men and women in the fields, and two big oxen that pulled a plough. I had never seen oxen before, or lizards, or the different kinds of insects that seemed to be everywhere. But the freedom of this mountain place was heady.

The walk to San Andrea was fun, and we sang and laughed on the way. At the first bend on the road, we reached a graveyard. Even that was different to what I was used to. They weren't underground, but in rows and rows of tiers in the wall, like a little town. Pictures of the dead were on each grave. My mother led us up the many stone steps until we came to her mother's grave. This was the first time I had seen a picture of my grandmother. She was so young and pretty and looked like my aunt Anastasia. I felt my mother's sadness (Children are pretty sensitive to feelings). When we left she was pretty quiet, but as we approached our destination she began to tell us something about where we were going, and that there were children at the house we were visiting.

San Andrea couldn't really be called a village. It was one of the many hamlets that were dotted here and there. There were about a dozen houses and a lot of land. We stopped at the second house. It was very big, and had a balcony in the middle of the first floor. A woman was standing, waving at us, and to my delight she spoke English. The man was very tall; he must have been the only tall man in the area, as everyone else we saw was small. There were three children, two boys and a girl. The eldest boy was the same age as me, and during our stay we all became friends. Little did I know then, but many years later he was to become my husband.

The games they played were very unusual, to say the least. They used to find bullets left over from the war and would put them in the ground, aim a rock at the top, and they would explode. Another favourite was to dig a hole and put solid gas under a tin that was propped up by a stick, tie a string to the stick, move back a bit, and then set fire to the string, which acted like a fuse. The tin can would fly up in the air a good few feet. He and his friends would go fishing in the river with sticks of dynamite they found lying about. Don't ask me how they ever grew up without killing themselves. If the adults had known the games we were playing, I don't think we would have been able to stand up for a week. But then, this was a grim reminder that a terrible war had taken place here and that nothing would ever be the same again. This hamlet had changed, and so had its inhabitants.

Angelina Magliocco, their mother, had been born in Ireland in 1914. She was a pretty woman, curvy, with shoulder-length wavy chestnut hair, and dark eyes. She was my first cousin, I was told. The daughter of my father's sister Rosa, she, along with her brothers and sisters, had spent a lot of her childhood in Casale with her maternal grandmother and her aunt Emilia. She returned to Ireland in her early teens, but couldn't seem to settle there. She missed the outdoor life and sunshine of the village. Her father was pretty strict with the girls and she wasn't allowed out much and so, in her early twenties, she decided to return to Italy. Her grandmother had since died, so she shared the family home with her spinster aunt. A few years later she married Alfonso, a young man from the hamlet of San Andrea. He was the only son of three children, whose father Salvatore had left the valley around 1912 with his brother Camillo, to seek their fortune in America. They were doing well, so well that he requested permission to bring his family there. He was granted the same in August 1915, by the City of New York, but tragedy was to bring about a change of destiny. His eldest daughter Rosa, Alfonso's sister, was stricken with TB, a disease that was rife at that time. He returned home, and Rosa died two years later. She was just nine years old.

* * *

The house in San Andrea was a thriving business. The downstairs rooms were a 'cantina' and grocery shop, and across the road they baked bread, pizzas and biscuits, which they sold in the shop. The wine was homemade, using their own homegrown grapes. In this manner, Alfonso managed to make a good living for his family. Salvatore had died suddenly of a heart attack in 1940, six months after the birth of his first grandson, Silvano. Angelina's father, Carmine, had died the same year. Both were sixty-two years old.

When the war arrived at this hamlet, the house was confiscated by the Germans, to accommodate the soldiers, as were all the houses in the area. The families were given twenty-four hours to evacuate. Angelina was distraught and terrified. At this time, she was pregnant with her third child. Her husband, along with men and boys of the area, had already been hiding in the higher mountains for months, sneaking down at night for food and warmth and a change of clothes. The wives used to signal to them by hanging sheets on the line a certain way, so they would know when it was safe to come down. Someone betrayed them and they were caught. A few tried to run away and were shot. The Commandant of the area where Alfonso was, was Austrian, and he allowed him to labour in the area. Others were sent to far off countries, and many never returned.

Angelina found a couple of rooms in a stable, high up on top of the mountain, past Montattico. She shared the place with another family. She took the top loft, and the other family the ground area. It was here, assisted by her sister-in-law Giuseppa, that she gave birth to her first daughter, Anna, on 30th November, 1943. She was to spend the next two years in this mountain stable, foraging for food, every day trying to keep her two young boys safe; and helping to feed the other children that were constantly hungry. She often went without food herself. A new young mother helped her to feed her own new baby, as her own milk dried up early. Through those freezing winter months, their only heat was from an ever-burning fire in the middle of the stable, the smoke of which was always present. They cooked on open fires and washed in streams. Overhead, there was a constant roar of hundreds of planes on their way to bomb Cassino, and more than once she saw men coming down in parachutes being gunned down and screaming as they floated in space. Their bedding was sacks stuffed with hay. Her footwear was an old pair of army boots that had been found on the road. Hunger was her constant companion.

One day, news reached them that the war was over, so they made their way back down the mountain to the village, and home. They were grouped with other people as they reached the bottom of the mountain, and found soldiers waiting to escort them back, as many mines had been planted around and about. The soldiers were speaking English – they were American – so Angelina asked a question. When they heard she could speak English, they asked her to go with them, to translate for them. Her mother-in-law was horrified. Not understanding what they wanted with her daughter-in-law, she started to scream. Finally, she understood, but was still nervous about letting her go. Angelina was gone for most of the day. Her job was to tell the people that the war was over and to get them to walk between the white tape that was lined on either side of the road. When she got back, her mother-in-law was delighted to see her. They were outside the house, as it was impossible to live in yet. There were lice and insects and dynamite, and all kinds of ammunition strewn around the place. No furniture, and potbelly stoves in every room; dirt and grime in every direction. So, they slept outside in the open for several weeks, until it was clean enough to live in. Everyone in the place pulled together to try to get some semblance of normality back. Alfonso, before the conflict, had started a haulage business and had two big lorries on the road. These had been confiscated and were long gone. There was nothing left. All their belongings were destroyed or robbed, houses were damaged, and devastation was all around. Vines were ruined, and there was nothing with which to start over. Later, Alfonso managed to get his hands on an old car and started a taxi service, but he never recovered enough to make his life there. Angelina gave birth to her second daughter, Luisa, in 1949. In 1950, they emigrated to Ireland. For a year, he could only get permission to stay for three months in the North, and then three months in the South, so he ferried back and forth between the borders until he finally got permission to stay in Dublin, through the help of his brother-in-law. The family settled in Cabra, Dublin, leaving behind Alfonso's elderly mother in the care of his sister.

* * *

The remainder of our stay that first summer was spent visiting various relations and friends, our eyes taking in the aftermath of the damage, especially in Cassino, which had been reduced to rubble. The lovely old Benedictine monastery perched high on the mountain-top overlooking the valley below, was no more. Thousands of young men now lay buried where they had fallen on its slopes; Poles, Jews, Americans, British, Germans and Italians, among them many civilians that were caught in the crossfire. That first visit to my mother's birth place left images that remain in my memory to this day.

Chapter Two
- Portadown -

Portadown, Co Armagh, in Northern Ireland was a large, thriving town with many factories, where most of the population found employment. My family had a café on the main street. It had taken my father many years of hard work to achieve this. He sold homemade ice-cream, fish and chips, tea, Bovril, Horlicks and soft drinks. The hours were long, and the work very labour intensive. Everything was done by hand. The ice-cream was boiled in a large copper container and stirred every so often with a large wooden paddle, much like an oar. This mixture was then poured into stainless steel buckets and left to cool. It took a lot of years pushing a cart around the streets, selling the ice-cream, before his dream became a reality. As children, we loved to go with our mugs and drink the hot mixture, which was then, in the early days, frozen in a barrel packed with dry ice, turned by a handle on the side. It was a slow process and we used to help take turns with turning the handle. The chips were also prepared by hand. Sacks of potatoes were washed with a hose, then peeled, eyed and chipped. This took up most of the early morning hours. It was a long, narrow shop and had nine 'snugs', or booths, downstairs. The second floor had twenty or more tables and chairs, to accommodate extra customers on busy days. The three bedrooms were also on the second floor and it was in one of these rooms that all three of us were born. Downstairs, just off the shop, was the large kitchen that housed a large, black, leaded range, on top of which four or five kettles of water were constantly on the boil, to supply the teas and Bovrils for the café. It was also used to cook the family meals. A table and chairs took up one corner, where we spent most of our day, doing homework, reading or listening to the radio. Our favourite radio programme at the time was *The Goons* show, a comedy starring Harry Secombe, Spike Milligan and Peter Sellers. Next to this kitchen was a second one that held a large, three-pan frying range with glass cabinets on top, to keep the fish and sausages hot. On from this was a preparation room and a store that held dry goods. Our playground was a large yard at the back of the premises that housed several outhouses. We passed many happy days in that yard, my brother and I, inventing most of the games we played. One favourite was a war game. We used the milk churns at either end of the yard as our fortresses, and with old saucepans on our head, and bin lids as armour, we would cheerfully get our 'ammunition' ready, which was anything we could get our hands on – rotten apples, or old potatoes – and fling them at each other. Sometimes we would go to the playground or the 'pleasure gardens' as they were called then, and spend many happy hours on the swings, roundabout and maypoles. It was in these gardens that the air-raid shelters were located. Every member of each household was allocated a gas mask. Babies had special ones they were placed in, like little carrycots with a glass window. The adults and older children's masks were pulled over the head. They had a longish hose in front, almost like an elephant's trunk, only shorter, and were carried in small cardboard boxes, with a string that slipped over your head. A siren would sound and people would run to the air-raid shelters complete with gas mask, but thankfully the planes would pass on, probably to drop their bombs on Belfast, the city sixty miles from us.

Although this part of Ireland was at war – being a part of the UK – business was booming, as the soldiers – in particular the Americans – were sent here to train before being shipped overseas. As a result, they would spend all their pay in the area, often giving the local children chocolate and chewing gum, and throwing coins as they passed by. All the houses and businesses had to adhere to the blackout rules, which meant thick black curtains hung at every window to stop any light spilling out onto the streets. As a result, at dusk the streets were pitch black. The café was lit by low gas lights and my mother told us many couples came in who had met outside, to see what each other looked like. Rationing was also introduced and each family were given books of coupons, one for clothing and one for sweets or sugar – one book per person. I still remember buying sweets with these coupons, as rationing continued for some years. Many women would donate some of their sweet coupons to young couples who were getting married, so they could have a small wedding cake; and often their clothes coupons too, to help towards a wedding outfit. White weddings were very rare and most young women were married in suits or simple dresses. Ice-cream could no longer be produced as it took too much sugar, butter and milk to make it. Instead of fresh milk, cans of condensed milk were used, and tins of corned beef replaced fresh meat, which was hard to procure. People lined up for hours at the butchers only to end up with a few sausages if they were lucky. Life seemed to be full of queues; for the baker, the butcher or the grocer. Tea was like gold dust, and the leaves were used over and over again.

Most of the young men were in the forces and so, for the first time, many women had to learn skills that previously had been male-oriented only, in order to keep things working. Prior to this, women mainly stayed at home to look after the family. It was considered bad for a woman to have to go to work, so they did jobs like taking in washing or ironing, to earn extra money for the large family that was the norm. The war changed this, and women learned to drive cars and lorries, operate machinery in the various factories, and generally take over jobs that had belonged to the man of the house. This caused a bit of conflict when the men returned and the woman had to give up jobs they had come to love, and were good at. This was to be the beginning of change in the women's role in society. My mother learned how to run the business while my father was interned. I often secretly thought she must have found it hard to hand over the reins when he returned.

There were few people who owned cars. Bicycles were the main means of transport, and horses and carts brought coal to the houses and served as transport for bringing goods to and fro. The majority walked everywhere. The rag and bone man, on his rounds, would call out to the children to bring jam jars in exchange for balloons. Even the cinemas would accept two jam jars as payment for admittance. The kids would scrounge around trying to find them so they could go to the pictures on a Saturday afternoon. There were three cinemas in the town, and it was the main form of entertainment. One of these cinemas always seemed to have Westerns showing, so we nicknamed it 'The Ranch'. Saturday afternoons at the Ranch were deafening as all the kids used to enter into the spirit of it, yelling when the Indians were attacking their favourites; Roy Rogers, the Cisco Kid, the Lone Ranger, Tom Mix; and cheering when their heroes won. Cowboys and Indians was by far the most favourite game of that time. Rounders (similar to baseball) was another favourite, and handball too. All the games were played on the street. The girls used to tie a rope around the lamppost and swing around it. We played conkers, marbles and skipping. The women used to sit outside their front doors, watching the kids at play, knitting socks or darning jumpers that always wore out at the elbows, chatting and catching up with the news. This was usually on Saturdays. They would exchange bits of leftover wool with each other, which was turned into very colourful jumpers. Nothing was thrown out or wasted.

We kids were always sent on errands, usually to the dairy shop for a quart or a pint of milk, and pats of butter, or a can of buttermilk for baking. Dairy shops don't exist today. Milk came in big silver churns, and we had cans with lids on them. The milk was ladled into the cans, and butter was sold in big soft pats, which were later with the help of two wooden pats – much like ping pong bats – rolled into little balls. They also sold fresh hen eggs or duck eggs, as well as stocking big, round cheese, from which one could buy a wedge. Or, we were sent to the corner shop which sold groceries and Woodbine cigarettes, the most popular brand at the time as they were the cheapest and the strongest. Another, slang name for these fags was 'coffin nails.' These shops had a slate on the wall for the purpose of giving credit. The names and amounts owed were recorded there, hence the term, 'Put it on the slate.' Snuff was also a popular item on the list, especially with the older women and men. This was a white, powdery substance, a pinch of which was placed on the back of the hand, then sniffed up the nostrils. With the arrival of supermarkets, these corner shops disappeared. Unlike today, shops of the era could only sell what they traded in. Butchers, for instance, could only sell meat, and grocery shops couldn't sell meat or dairy products. Hats were sold at the milliners shop; garages sold cars and petrol, etc. In a way, it was fairer than today, and less competitive.

When rationing ended, we started to make ice-cream again. We couldn't keep up with the demand. People brought their own bowls and bought it by the scoop. Some children who were born during these years were tasting it for the first time. Wafers, or 'sliders', were the most popular. This was two wafer biscuits with ice-cream in the middle, and one slid their tongue all around the edges, hence the name 'sliders.' We used two different stamps to make the wafers.

In 1947, my parents bought a private house on the edge of town, just a few hundred yards from the convent school I attended. With the birth of my sister, Rina, it had gotten a bit cramped living in the Café Rex. The new house had five bedrooms, two living rooms, a dining room, a large kitchen and a laundry room that housed the first washing machine we ever had. It was a big, round drum with a mangle on top. At this same time, my mother employed a housekeeper nanny, to look after us while she went to the shop with my father. Her name was Peggy. A young woman from Coalisland, County Tyrone, she was a wonderful person and treated us like her own children, especially Rina who was only a baby when she arrived. She was always singing the Vera Lynn songs, White Cliffs of Dover, Lili Marlene; It's a Long Way to Tipperary, and rebel songs too. Although we were Italian, we learnt quite a few of them. When she wasn't singing, she would talk to the pots and pans, laughingly telling us to start worrying when the pots and pans started answering her back. She loved to dress my sister up in her prettiest dresses and would curl her baby hair with a lotion called 'Curly Top'. She was one of those rare people who had a great love for all children, and they in turn always responded to her. She often joined in on our games, especially the skipping ones. There she would be in the middle of the street, jumping in and out of the rope like a ten-year-old. She stayed a part of our family for many years, even after she married and had children of her own.

We soon settled into a routine in the new house. My brother Mario was always first up; he would light the fire and make my father and mother an espresso coffee before he went to school. I, on the other hand, was always the last up, having a problem with mornings – I still have, to this day. My energy seemed to come at night, so my family nicknamed me the Night Owl. As a result of this, I was always late for school, even though it was just a few hundred yards away and you could see it from the house. It didn't do to be late for school, because the cane was always waiting for latecomers and it was a slap for every minute you were late. It was also a slap for every spelling you got wrong, every sum you got wrong, and, as we used pen and ink, every blot on the page. Ponytails were forbidden; plaits were the most acceptable. Each letter you wrote had to be the same size. Cane and I got to know each other very well at this time. The truant officer came around once a month to inspect the roll book. If you were late even by five minutes you were marked absent, so the poor guy asked me why I wasn't in school for a whole month. I told him I was, but as I was late, they marked me absent. He did try to be nice and asked me how far I lived from the school. The nun took great delight in marching him to the window to show him. Result: My parents got fined. Ah, well! It kept the class laughing for many a day.

This was the only Catholic girls' school in the town and it was badly overcrowded. There were classes even in the summer houses in the school grounds. The same nun taught the class all the subjects, and as I pointed out to my sister many years later, either the nun was a genius or we learnt very little. Some classrooms had three different years in them. The other schools were open to us, but if you attempted to go to even the technical school, you would hear about it from the priest, who by the way lived beside us. My brother didn't fare much better as he had the Christian Brothers, and often came home with his hands cut from the leather straps they used. And if your hands were alright, your ears were often ringing from being pulled or being slapped on the side of the head. Or, the ruler would make a good job of your knuckles. These being the only Catholic schools, there was no choice but to stay, or so I thought. People were very mannerly then. Men would raise their hats or caps to women, and children would never dream of answering their elders back.

Every Thursday, my parents would close the shop and this was our family day. We usually went visiting relations and friends who lived in the neighbouring towns, or to Belfast, to the cinema, or pantomimes. They had many friends in the city, who were from the same village in Italy. As a matter of fact, most of the Italians in Ireland are from the same area. Portstewart always took priority, as my mother loved to visit my maternal grandfather who was now living with his eldest daughter. They were extremely close as he had been both father and mother to them. Most Christmases we spent there, as he had a heart condition and couldn't travel. My mother did all the cooking as she loved nothing better than cooking all the wonderful traditional Italian dishes. She would spend hours making a special honey cake, that unfortunately I never learnt to do. In the evening we would play Tombola, or Bingo as it's known in Ireland. They made this holiday especially lovely, as the shop was closed for a few days, and we could all be together. I have always loved Christmas, and still do, perhaps because it is always a reminder of a lovely childhood.

* * *

It was one of these visits that was the catalyst for my being sent to boarding school for a few years. My mother must have been complaining about the local school to her sister, when she suggested sending me to St Mary's Dominican Convent in Portstewart. This was a two-hour journey from where we lived. It was then a private school, and they thought it would be better for me as there were already four Italian girls there that we knew. Big mistake. All I really remember of that episode was being very homesick and crying most nights along with all the other girls in my dorm; including, might I add, the famous four who were already in there. Two of these girls were sisters, the youngest being only four or five. Her name was Frances, she had golden curly hair and was a lovely child. Her sister was nine or ten, called Lena. Somehow, these two stuck in my memory, even though I honestly don't remember much else about that period. What I do remember is they were not treated very nice, especially the little girl. She would have accidents at night and they were made wash the sheet for punishment. I think the little girl had a kidney problem, but I couldn't be sure – memory sometimes can play tricks.

We only got home for the holidays; Easter, Christmas and the summer. The rest of the time we weren't allowed out, except on Sunday afternoons in a long 'crocodile' formation, escorted by two nuns. We had to keep our eyes straight ahead, but were allowed to talk to each other. When visitors came, a nun remained in a corner of the room, so we couldn't really talk. We were woken at 7am by a bell clanging in our ears, had to wash and tidy the cubicle and the bed, and then go to Mass, before we were allowed to go to the dining room for breakfast, then on to class. The tummies that rumbled those mornings were like a symphony. I left that place after three years, convincing my father to let me come home during a time my mother had gone to Italy with Mario and Rina. He was a soft man and couldn't bear to leave me there so distraught, so there and then he told the sisters to pack my things, and I went home. My mother wasn't impressed with his decision. I always wondered what happened the two girls and, many years later – in fact only in 2001, in the piazza in Casale – I got talking to a young girl. It turned out, to my delight, that she was the daughter of Lena, but that sadly, Frances had died when she was young. I started to tell the girl what I had remembered of the convent. She looked at me in astonishment; told me her mother had told them for years what they had gone through, but they had thought she was exaggerating, until my story confirmed it. Frances had died from kidney failure – it seems she did have a kidney problem after all - and Lena suffered from bouts of depression. I hope my verifying her story has helped in some way. She also told me that Lena was in the charismatic movement in Belfast, a Christian prayer movement through which I too have since found great blessings.

* * *

Shortly after this episode, Angelina and her family arrived in Portadown. They moved in with her mother who had a café at the opposite end of the town from us. It was my job to collect Anna, who was seven years old, and bring her to school with me. She didn't speak English and was very shy. The nun had her tell the names of things in Italian and sing a song. Her brothers went to the boys' school and, after three months, they all had a good command of the language. As young people do, they soon settled in and made friends. Each summer holiday, the school children were recruited to help the farmers bring in their harvest. Some went to the fruit farms and some went to the famous McGredy rose nursery, to help prune the roses that were sent to England and other places. I worked on the fruit farm picking gooseberries and loganberries, for which I was paid a halfpenny a punnet. Buses collected us at the boys' school and we were all given a label with our names and numbers on them – mine was 126. It was brilliant fun and we could eat as much as we wanted plus earn a few pennies to buy gobstoppers and sweets. The fruit we picked went to the jam factory. Looking back, it was a good way to speed up production, and was a very healthy way to pass the summer; plus, all the children got free milk and orange juice. Many of these children gave their earnings to their mothers. In those days, hire-purchase was non-existent, so to buy anything, one needed cash. A lot of the older generation were illiterate, and many families had great hardship, especially as most couples had a large number of children, living in 'two up, two down' terraced houses, so the head of the house had often to go to England to find work, and send money back. We were often asked to read letters and answer them to the owner's dictation.

* * *

I finished out my schooldays in the Convent in Portadown. When I was fourteen years old I left, as did most of the young people at that time, and started work with my parents. Mario, my brother, continued his education at St Patrick's College in Armagh, a town thirty miles away. Portadown didn't have a second level school, neither for boys nor girls. As second level at that time wasn't free, most families that could afford it sent their sons on, plus some who were lucky enough to win a scholarship. Mario was amazing in a way. He was born left-handed and this was considered abnormal, so they used to tie his left hand behind his back and force him to use his right one. As a consequence, he was able to write with both hands equally well, and often had two copies in front of him, writing away. This was especially useful for doing the many lines that were dished out for punishment. Everybody had a wireless. Ours was on a high shelf in the kitchen, and Mario would perch on the back of a chair so he could get closer, and would do his homework in this manner every day.

School wasn't his favourite place, so after a lot of mitching and absences, he threw in the towel and left at sixteen, and came to work in the Café. We all enjoyed working together and couldn't have been in a better place, as all the teenagers and all our friends came in every night. Pubs weren't in vogue at that time. Women never went into pubs – it was considered shameful – and the few who did couldn't drink in the main bar where the men were. There was a snug portioned off at the end of the bar, and they were served through a little hatch. So, a night out was cinema once a week, then into the cafes for lemonade or ice-cream, tea, Bovril or milkshakes. Coffee was unheard of then. So, in the café we heard all the gossip and discussed the latest hit songs. Our day started at 11am and finished at 11pm, but we had lots of breaks in between. The same year I left school, my father sold the house and we moved back to Café Rex. He had renovated the old place, removed the café upstairs, and created a bigger flat. We had three bedrooms, a large living room and an ample kitchen, a small laundry room and a good-sized bathroom. It was much easier to live and work under the same roof, especially for my mother, as we were all together, and she could spend more time with us; and my younger sister, who was seven, needed her to be there. Mammy was a jolly person, laughed a lot and loved visitors. She was an excellent cook and everything was homemade, I don't ever remember eating anything tinned. She had always some project going, either her crochet or embroidery. Her linens were always snow-white and the house immaculate. There was always someone calling to see her. Both my parents spoke English with an accent, and sometimes the words would come out wrong and we would have a good laugh, like when my mother wanted a bottle of hair lacquer she would pronounce it 'lager' and then get mad when she was presented with a bottle of beer; or she would call our male cook and ask him if he would do a massage for her, instead of a message. We would keep her going for days. Peggy had left to get married but still called in regularly. Mammy liked good clothes and always looked stylish. She had a good circle of friends, both Irish and Italian, so our flat was always busy. My father, on the other hand, was quiet and calm, and the two personalities complimented each other nicely. We were a family of five, two adults, three children, two girls and a boy, the middle girl being myself, two years and two weeks younger than my brother, and eight years senior to my little sister. My brother Mario and I were closer than twins.

My sister Rina looks like my mother's family but has more of my father's character, while my brother and I are the reverse.

Chapter Three
- On Pilgrimage -

It was decided I was to accompany my father and uncles to Italy. This was my second trip. The men's purpose was more in the form of a pilgrimage. During the war years they had promised that if all the family got through the war safely they would make the journey to Lourdes, and then on to San Giovanni to see a young friar who had the stigmata.

This time, we made the journey by car. We took the ferry from Belfast to Liverpool and drove down to Dover, where we got a second ferry to Calais. The trip was boring; all those hours in the car, not really interested in what the men were talking about. We stayed in Lourdes for two or three days. It was a lovely experience. We drank the waters and took some with us, then made our way to Italy. Things looked a lot better in the five years of my absence and, being older, I took more interest in what I was seeing. A lot of rubble had been cleared and new buildings were standing in place of the old. Roads and bridges were restored so we made good progress, arriving at our home village mid-afternoon. This was my father's first trip in fifteen years. To me, nothing in the village had changed since my last trip; the roads were still gravelly, the women still had their baskets on their heads and still did their washing in the river. The only thing that struck me was the presence of a lot more livestock on the farms than before. My aunt was the proud owner of a pig, her garden was full of many vegetables, and her store room was well stocked. Legs of ham hung from hooks on the ceiling and, best of all, there was electricity, but just for light. There was still no machinery in the fields, and the oxen were out in force. A few of the villagers had some sheep that had to be brought up the mountain every morning, and the shepherds always stayed with them until they brought them back in the evening; the bells that hung around their necks making a merry noise to signal their whereabouts. They are never left alone up there because of the wolves that roam about the higher peaks. Because it was September, the grapes were being harvested, and I enjoyed helping to pick the juicy bunches and throw them into the wicker baskets that were then loaded on to donkeys and brought to the wine press. The juice was then left to ferment. It was hard work but enjoyable, and everyone was in a good mood and sang and told stories all the while they worked. Corn was also harvested, and it was a joint effort. The village women would gather the sheaves of corn into a barn and strip the leaves off them, throwing the yellow corn into baskets, which were then shared out. This was used mainly to feed the chickens. Tomatoes were pushed into bottles with some basil leaves, capped and boiled in large drums, and some were spread on trays to dry and thicken in the sun, for the making of the tasty sauces that made the various pastas so delicious. It was a very busy month for the village; wood also had to be cut and stored for the cold winter months ahead.

* * *

The way to San Giovanni was long, and the journey took us four hours. It was a little village on top of a hillock. We had to leave the car pretty far from the little church where the priest who had the stigmata, Padre Pio, was to say Mass. There were crowds of people and, don't ask me how, but we managed to get into the church. We were standing against the wall directly opposite the confessional where, before Mass, the Padre was hearing confessions. Some people angered him and he refused them absolution. My aunt wanted me to go, but after seeing this I declined. I didn't understand at the time, but it was explained to us that he could tell whether a person was truly repentant or not. I was too afraid to approach him, sure that all my sins were on show. During the Mass, there was a beautiful smell that I thought was flowers. The priest's hands bled during the consecration, and the smell was coming from there. When he held up the

Host it was like he was somewhere else. He stayed in that position for what must have been a full fifteen minutes. The same happened when he raised the Chalice. When Mass ended he went outside and blessed all the people. In a way, this affected me more than Lourdes had. My father had kept his promise.

The following Sunday, there was a grand festa in Casale. A band arrived in the square, and there was Mass followed by a procession all around the village. We followed the statue of Our Lady, singing and praying; people from all the hamlets gathered together. Coloured lights lit up the streets, stalls with little toys and food were set up that night, and everyone danced to an accordion in the Piazza. It finished at midnight with a fireworks display. It was a wonderful day, a marvellous end to our holiday. Back home, everyone in the Italian community was getting ready to go to the annual dress dance in Belfast's Orpheus Ballroom.

Chapter Four

- Socialising -

My brother and I were very excited. This was our first dance, and my father was taking us. The men hired dinner suits, or 'monkey suits' as we used to call them. I was just turned sixteen, and the preparation for it was tinged with excitement. My dress was an organza creation; the background was green with large pink flowers patterned on it, and it was dotted here and there with gold spots. It had a full skirt that reached my ankles, and I complemented it with gold shoes and a gold purse. It also had a stole of matching material. To finish my ensemble I added a pair of short, white gloves. I describe it because, you're right, it was gaudy! I styled my hair in the Jane Wyman cut, flat to my head with a fringe. Of course, at the time I thought I was the bee's knees. To this day it gives my sister and I great cause for mirth. The ballroom had a lovely polished floor, and a large ball turned in the centre of the ceiling, casting lovely colours around the dimly-lit room. The dances of the day were foxtrots, quicksteps, samba, cha-cha and the Gay Gordons, and beautiful Strauss waltzes. We girls all knew the different steps but most of the boys didn't, so our feet suffered from constant treading on or stumbling over. The only problem with this kind of dancing was you needed a partner. It was at this dance that my brother met his wife, Angelina, for the first time. She lived in Newry, a town thirty miles from ours. I met nobody, and no wonder; my dress would have blinded anyone from ten paces. Nevertheless, it was very enjoyable. My father even enjoyed talking to the other fathers who had escorted their children.

* * *

One morning, I got up to the sound of men's voices huffing and puffing as they carried a cabinet up the stairs. My father wouldn't let us into the living room for a few hours, and kept saying it was a surprise. My brother and I couldn't understand why all the fuss over a cabinet. He waited until we were all together, then called us into the room. The cabinet stood in the corner of the room, a nice piece of furniture. We had to close our eyes, and when we opened them, we were left with our mouths open. It was a *television!* The excitement was contagious and we were all talking at the same time, asking questions. I still remember vividly the utter amazement as the pictures flashed on the screen. We had our own cinema in the house! Our staff came up to see it, as well as neighbours and friends; it was a miracle of the times. With it came good and bad. People didn't visit each other as much, and it killed conversation. Women no longer sat outside their doors on a Saturday, and children slowly but surely dropped the street games. On the positive side, the outside world was brought into the homes, and with it an awareness of the misery some nations were suffering. TV became the focus of family life. It also interfered with our time spent in the Café. My brother and I would often argue over whose turn it was to watch the 'Six-Five Special', a programme solely dedicated to show bands. My father no longer went to the cinema; there was no need. And, for a period of years, many cinemas had to close down. In our own town, only one remained open. Many other changes were creeping in, especially on the music front, from sedate ballroom dancing and romantic love songs to the mad, crazy world of rock and roll. Elvis 'The Pelvis' Presley rocked the youth of the world, overnight. All us young people spent every spare moment teaching each other how to jive. The Ballrooms were horrified, the clergy were horrified, parents were horrified. They did everything in their power to stop it. Dance halls hired people especially to stop the jiving and rock and rolling, and it was banned in most of these places. The few that allowed it had queues trying to get in. The style of dress changed dramatically. Boys wore 'teddy boy' suits, long jackets with velvet lapels, pink shirts, drainpipe trousers, and hair styles plastered with oily lotion shaped into a duck's tail at the back. Girls, on the other hand, wore circular skirts with three of four frilly petticoats underneath, broad elastic belts, flat black shoes, bobby socks and outrageous hairdos. The beehive was a favourite, piled so high that knitting needles had to be used if you needed to scratch your head. One day while I was fixing my beehive, which involved backcombing the hair until it looked like a bird's nest, then smoothing the outer layer around and fastening it with lots of hair pins; to save time I was using the mirror in the living room. Suddenly, my father, who was observing this, asked me what I was trying to do with myself. When I replied that I was combing my hair, he nearly hit the roof! Things had certainly changed. Everyone started to smoke in secret, choking on every puff, but determined to look as if they were 'cool cats', and not 'squares'. My poor father, observing us jiving one day, told us we were like a bunch of wild Indians. But nobody listened, they couldn't stop it. We teenagers were flying on the crest of change. When the Beatles hit the music scene, there was no stopping us. Unlike Elvis, these lads were dressed more conservatively with dark suits and hair bobs. From duck's tail hair do's, the trend switched to smooth bobs. Every young lad now had this look, except the poor guys who had the misfortune to have curly, frizzy hair. The girls, on the other hand, had short, backcombed hair with kiss-curls around the face. To achieve this look, girls with dead straight hair would use sugar and water to hold the kiss curls in place. This was fine until the sugar dried and you were left with white dots that looked like dandruff. Skirts were so pencil-slim and tight at the bottom that it made walking on four-inch stiletto heel shoes, with long pointed toes, a trifle difficult. Running was out of the question, and those that attempted it looked anything but elegant, to say nothing of the bunions a lot of us possess today thanks to this type of footwear. Fashion has a lot to answer for, don't you think? My father sure wasn't impressed!

* * *

Periodically throughout our childhood, my brother and I would go to visit my father's brother in Dublin, Angelo Cafolla, who was the eldest boy of the family. He lived with his wife Lucia and their six children in the Fairview Café on Annesley Bridge Road, a busy thoroughfare just a twenty minute bus ride from the city centre. They were a lovely family and I always enjoyed going there for a week or two. I had great fun with my cousins in Fairview. There were three boys – Nino, Fulvio and Gerry; and three girls – Maria, Esterina and Anna. They were all grown up and, as I was younger, they made a big fuss of me.

The girls shared a bedroom that had a gas fire on the wall and, every night, we would all sit on the floor around the gas fire while Esterina would read a book to us. 'Little Women' was my favourite. Or, we would chat and they would share stories and general gossip, or curl my hair. I remember Maria was the glamorous one of the trio. She looked like a film star and had a boyfriend in Italy. His name was Dino Fusco, he was tall and handsome, and they were writing to each other. She would read us some bits of his letters, and they were so romantic. She went on to marry him and they had four boys and two girls. Esterina had something wrong with her eyes and wore glasses. She was small, had dark hair and a wonderful personality. She was also very witty and would have us in stitches laughing. She always gave out about her boyfriend buying her toffee, as it would stick to her false teeth and give her bother. She married Roger Cervi, had three children – a boy and two girls – and emigrated to Los Angeles, America. Her son, Larry, while training for the police force, fell badly and broke his neck. He was paralysed from the shoulders down, at twenty-four years of age.

Anna was outgoing, the youngest of the family, very chatty and full of life, a very pretty girl. She married Bernardo Gentile and had three children. Nino, the eldest, was of average size, dark-haired and good looking. He married a Dublin girl called Nell and started a business doing wrought iron.

Fulvio had the looks of Rossano Brazzi, a popular film star of that era. He moved to Leeds in England, married Anna Maria and had one daughter. Gerry was also good looking. He went to Indiana in America, married and settled there. They were full of mischief. I remember they had an air-gun that shot little pellets, and they would shoot tin-can targets. One day his sister Maria was in the yard and he opened his bedroom window and asked her to hold up her thumb, which she did, and by some freak accident the pellet actually hit it. Needless to say there were fun and games when Uncle Angelo found out. The gun was confiscated. They had an Alsatian dog, and we would walk along the sea-front to Dollymount Strand and back. They took me everywhere with them.

* * *

During the summer of 1954, I met my first boyfriend. His name was Don. He was tall, dark and average looking, and worked in McGredy's nursery shop, which was directly across the road from the Café Rex. We were both fifteen and very shy. He would come into the café at every opportunity, but it took a good few weeks before he plucked up the courage to ask me out. This, for me, was a major problem, as I was only allowed out one day a week and had to be in by 10pm; and, under no circumstances was I allowed to see boys. So, I had to refuse, but he persisted until I finally agreed. I couldn't go to the cinema, however, as all the staff there knew me and came into the café, so I dared not take the chance in case it got back to my mother's ears. With the help of my best friend Eileen I managed to meet him at 6:30pm, as far away from the town centre as I could. She agreed to meet me at 9pm and come back home with me so my parents would see I was with her. That first date, we went for a walk. He was a really nice person, and we met like this once a week for many months. There was a lot of innocence in those days. Couples kissed and held hands and that was the height of it. Everything had to pass a censor board before it was released to the public; films, books, newspapers and magazines, radio. No bad language or saucy pictures were allowed anywhere. Drugs hadn't yet hit the scene, sex was never mentioned, and our generation grew up totally ignorant of the facts of life. We had many discussions among ourselves trying to figure out this great mystery, and never coming up with the right answer. Mothers would tell their daughters the day before their wedding.

A girl's biggest fear was having a baby out of wedlock. There was an awful stigma attached to it; they were considered terrible sinners, ostracised by society. The children also carried the shame by having the title 'bastard' attached to their names. Indeed, these poor innocent children suffered terrible insults. It's hard to imagine today the serious repercussions of such a thing at that time. The girl would be sent to some kind of home, never to be seen again. Some courageous families kept their girls, and their babies suffered the same treatment from neighbours and friends and clergy. A lot of the girls were forced to marry men who volunteered to wed them, but the ceremony was always carried out in the sacristy – a side room off the main church. These became known as 'shotgun' weddings.

Don and I were seeing each other whenever I could safely sneak a date, but eventually we were caught – and all hell broke loose in both families. He was a Protestant, and I Catholic. Both families did their utmost to break up the relationship. Our generation were quite liberal about religious differences, and often had long discussions about it, but the older generation wouldn't tolerate a match of this kind. Sometimes a young man or woman would convert to marry, but these were considered turncoats and shunned by their original peers. Those were difficult days for my family; there were constant arguments in the house, each one refusing to bow to the other's will. It only served to make us more determined to see each other – and see each other we did – until the romance died a natural death, and peace reigned once more in Café Rex – for a while anyway.

* * *

Mario was what you would call the life and soul of the party. He was always very obliging and friendly to everyone he met, full of life, and very good to our mother. If she needed to go somewhere to visit her friends, he would always be ready to bring her. He wasn't very interested in going to dances when we were young, but would come with me, as I wasn't allowed go on my own. If I met a date at the dance he would wait for me at the top of our entry. One time, a dance was organised for the Italian football team that had been playing a match in Ireland. It was held in the Orpheus Ballroom in Belfast. Prior to the dance, Mario, being his usual obliging self, arranged to also take three Italian girls we knew well. So we set off, collected the girls on the way, and got ready to have a good time. All night, these girls would, in turn, approach me angrily and state they would never speak to Mario again, that he was just trying to make a fool of them. I was in the dark as to what their beef was about. In the end, I discovered that each one had thought they were going to be his special date for the night, whereas Mario had only been offering them a lift, and couldn't understand why none of them would speak to him. Shortly after this dance, however, he started to date Angelina Fallone.

Chapter Five
- Tying the Knot -

The Fallones came from Olivella, a farming area just a few miles from Cassino. Benedetto and his wife Giovanna moved a few times before they settled in Newry. Angelina was the youngest of five children, two of whom had emigrated to America. Her mother had unfortunately died in her early fifties of a sudden heart attack, two years before she and Mario had started to go out together. Her father never really got over it – they had been childhood sweethearts and had married when they were just eighteen years old. After two years of dating, Angelina and Mario themselves got married – in April, 1960 – and moved in with us until they bought a house of their own. Riccardo, their first born son, arrived in May of the following year. It was a great novelty having a baby in the family. I met another young man too – Art Boston – but, as luck would have it, he too was Protestant, so the same performance started again. Neither set of parents wanted the match, and war once more came to the Café Rex.

In the summer of that year I was shipped off to Portstewart, to work the summer in my aunt's café. She was even more strict than my mother, but with the help of my cousin Guido I managed to sneak out to a few dances, and barbecues on the beach, and all in all had a good time. My grandfather used to save my bacon as well, as he was always telling my aunt to leave me alone. I suppose my mother was hoping the break away would finish my romance. Not a hope. When I returned home, I would sneak off on dates with Art, but it was really a very hard time. I used to get so depressed at times, with all the arguments in the house. One morning before I got up, Mario appeared in my room with a train ticket to Dublin for me and a packed case. Someone was in the shop telling my mother she had seen me out the night before with Art Boston. Mario sneaked me out, and down to the train station. He couldn't bear to see my mother at me, so he arranged with my cousin Rita to let me stay for a week or two until the heat died down.

I liked Rita, and John, her husband. She was ten years older than me and very modern, so I was happy to go. Rita was small and petite. She played the piano very well and the three of us would sing all the old Neapolitan songs in the evening or go for a drive to Dollymount, singing all the way. I think my mother must have been even happier to have me there, what do you think? During this trip, I met up with Alfonso, Angelina and family. They had bought the café in Fairview from my uncle, who had retired, so it was great meeting up again with the family.

When I was ready to return to Portadown, Alfonso asked if I would help them out, as his staff had gone on strike. I told him he had to ask my parents, who agreed to my staying on until he got sorted. I stayed on for a month. I would go out with Silvano and his friends, who were children of other Italians that were from Casalattico. We had great fun, going to the roller rink in Bray, dances in the city, and generally hanging out. It was at this time that Silvano and I fell in love. I returned home, deciding not to say anything to my family as I wasn't sure if this romance was going to go anywhere. A few days later he called, asking if he could come up to see me. We met every second Tuesday. He would drive up from Dublin with two of his friends, Thomas and Sylvester. The three of us would go to Belfast, then split up until it was time to return home. They would leave the same night. This went on for a few months, before Silvano would stay overnight.

Eventually, as was the custom in those days, Silvano came up to ask my father if we could be married. A shy man, he spent a long time sweating nervously at the door of the kitchen – where inside my father was blissfully unaware of what was going on outside – trying to pluck up the courage to go in. Silvano told me afterwards that he had said to my father that he wanted to be engaged for a year, and to marry the following May, to which Dad had replied, "What's your hurry?" For some reason, as Silvano pointed out to me, Dad was reading the newspaper upside-down at the time. Hopefully this was not going to be an omen for our marriage! We got engaged in the most romantic of settings – the top deck of a double-decker bus in Dublin – and set the date of our wedding for the 1st May, 1962. We were nearly twenty-three when we married.

Ten days before the wedding, on a Good Friday, my grandfather died. It was a very sad time, and my mother and sister were overcome with grief, but in spite of this they wouldn't let me cancel the wedding. Angelina and Mario were expecting their second son within days of the wedding. He arrived a week later, so they named him Amedeo after our grandfather. It was strange. We had a death, a wedding and a birth, all within three weeks of each other. We left the wedding after the dinner – all our family did – to leave the guests dance the rest of the night away.

We spent our honeymoon driving to Italy via France, Spain and Switzerland. The journey was really lovely, and we had six weeks of holiday. We set up home in Glasnevin in Dublin. We had a fast-food shop with a house adjoined. It had four bedrooms, a small kitchen, and a living-cum-dining room. To make more room, Silvano decided to try his hand at carpentry and made a table that was attached to the wall with hinges and folding legs, so that it could be stored flat against the wall when not in use. The idea was great, but it was a bit hard to eat while holding up one end with your knees, as the legs weren't the same length. He didn't have much success tiling the floor either. We chose cream linoleum tiles, that were stuck down with a black glue. I think he overdid the glue, as the black stuff would keep leaking out for years afterwards. Those were strange days for me, trying to adjust to my new life. Although we were in the same kind of business, the hours were much later at night and most of our friends would call after work to play cards. We would be up until the early hours, and would sleep in until 2pm. The shop didn't open until five in the evening.

Married life was very different from what I had thought. For a start, cooking was a big problem for me as the kitchen was the last place you would have found me at home. Mammy would often call me to look at and learn all the lovely dishes she would make, but in true Maria form I would make my excuses and take off. So, the meals were a series of disasters, especially the first roast beef I tried making for my first dinner guests. When it was nice and brown outside, I assumed it was cooked until I cut it and was rewarded with raw, bloody flesh on the inside. I solved the problem by throwing it in the bin, and dished up a sorry looking omelette instead, complete with roast potatoes and peas. It was many months before I had a dinner party again. Washing clothes was my second nightmare; we didn't have a washing machine. Apart from that fact, at home we always had a daily helper who took care of all the chores, so now I would leave this job until we ran out of things to wear (probably hoping by some miracle they would wash themselves). Then, I would fill the bath, dump everything in, take off my shoes and stockings and sit on the edge of the bath, using my feet like an agitator, changing the water numerous times until we had no hot water left. This worked to a certain extent, but it took hours, so after several times of trying this, it dawned on me that it was better to do the washing every other day, since it seemed they were not going to clean themselves after all. It was also brought home to me how much I had taken my mother for granted, and how little I knew about running a home. This was on top of trying to get used to living with a partner who had different ways from mine. We had both grown up in different families and had to find our way together and, after many arguments, tears and frustrations, we learned the art of compromise.

Dublin city was a bit of a nightmare. When I first tried to go into town by myself – after living all of my life in a small town – getting the bus in was no problem, but on the way back I could never recognise my stop, especially if it was dark. More than once, I ended up back at Nelson's Pillar in the city centre, and had to do the whole journey all over again. Managing money was so hard too, it just wouldn't stretch the way it was supposed to. I was so used to spending my wages on clothes and make-up, never having to think about bills, that it took a while before I mastered it.

On Sundays, we closed the business, and it was on one of these Sundays that Silvano took me to visit a friend of his, who lived in a little two-roomed flat in Terenure. Her name was Antoinette, and she had just had a baby girl. She had married against her father's wishes and was estranged from her family. Silvano and her other Italian friends were helping her, and visited very often. We hit it off and became great friends, helping each other through many rough patches. More often than not, though, I would go home to Portadown on our day off, to get a little bit of pampering.

Photo time...

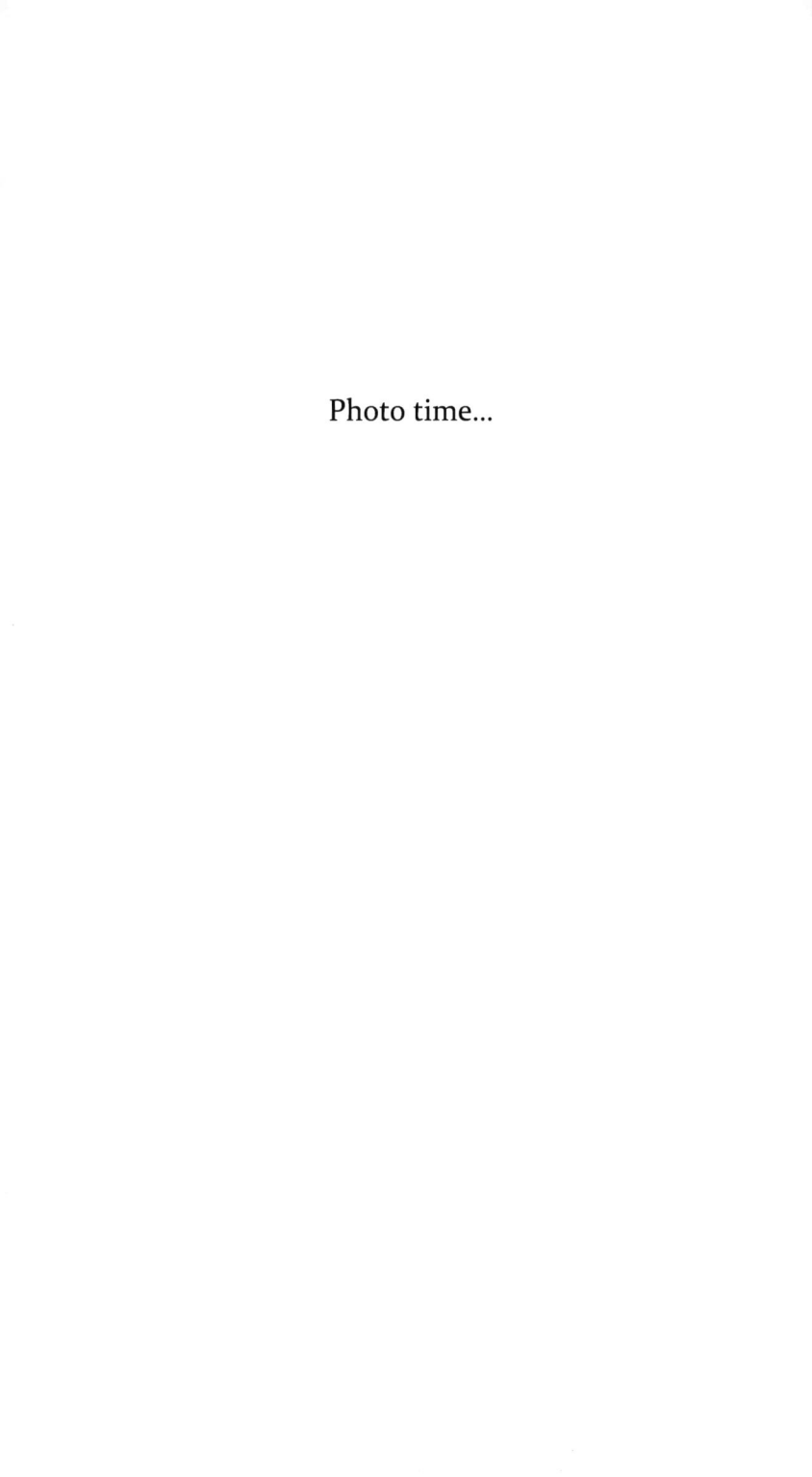

Mario, Mammy and I

Myself, Rina and Mario

My parents Rocco and Lidia Cafolla, with myself
and Mario

Silvano (tallest) with his siblings, and their
house in San Andrea

A visit to Emilia (centre)

Silvano's mother, Angelina

The terrible two again!

Stepping out with Silvano

With Silvano's father, Alfonso

Mum and I with Angela and the twins

Angie with Silvano jr
on the loggia in Fairview

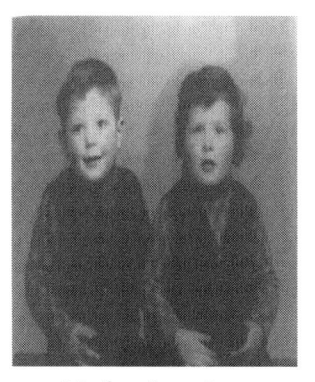

My lovely twins,
Sandro and Sandra

Angela's Holy Communion. With Silvano and Sandro

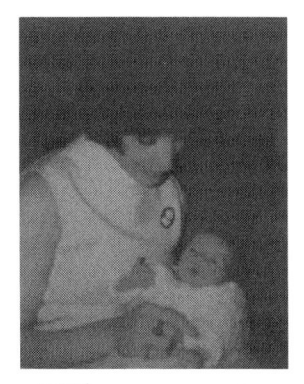

With my youngest,
Silvano jr

Family photo for Angela's
Confirmation

Rocco and Lidia Cafolla

Alfonso and Angelina Taddei

Another family photo, with my daughter-in-law
Paola and grandchildren Sara and Stefano

My fantastic four!

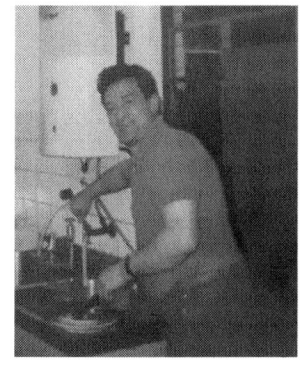

Mario working with us in
Killarney

Three of my grandchildren, Stefano, Chiara and Rocco

Lost between my grandson Clay and son-in-law Steve

Surrounded by love!

My granddaughter Sara and her husband Tom

My grandchildren Clay and Sabina

Silvano with his wife Viera and their children

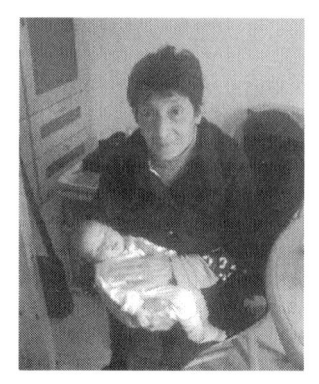

Proud Nonna with baby Chiara

Mario and Rina, my wonderful siblings

Two of many great moments with my lovely husband by my side

Chapter Six
- Early Days -

In July, I got pregnant with my first baby, but miscarried nine weeks later. After a short interval I got pregnant again. I was very nervous during this time, but the doctors assured me most women lose their first baby. Even so, I took great care during this nine months. The day before my due date, the baby died. It was a little boy, and the labour was very long. I was sedated a lot of the time, and as soon as I delivered him, they put me out. In the early Sixties, they didn't really consider babies who were stillborn, and I suppose they thought it was for the best if the mothers didn't see them, so he was whipped away and buried before I could get a glimpse of him, even though I had asked to see him. He is still in my heart, and I think of him every day. Because he didn't receive baptism, he was buried in a special plot in Glasnevin cemetery, which they now call the Angel plot. I was so depressed and heartbroken, in my head I decided I wouldn't try again, that it hurt too much. In spite of all my great intentions I conceived a few months later, but all during this pregnancy I didn't really think it would go well, and I was afraid for the baby the whole nine months. All my family and friends were worried for me.

Angelina was expecting her third child at the same time. Her and Mario's daughter was born in February. They named her Lidia, after my mother. I was a bit miffed. That was the name I was going to choose if I had a girl. On 17th May, 1964 I indeed gave birth to a healthy baby girl. She weighed 5lbs 14ozs, and was a forceps delivery as the cord had been around her neck. She came two weeks early. I couldn't believe the baby lived. We spent hours watching the miracle that was her. We named her Angelina Anna, but shortened it to Angela, then 'Angie'. My mother came to stay with me for a while after her birth as, true to form, I knew nothing about babies. It was great having her; she made everything look so easy, so much so that I didn't realise just how much she *was* doing, until she left. Angie was a good baby, but I had my L-plates on, so she had to put up with my inexperience. I must have been on the phone two or three times a day to my mother, every time she didn't do what it said in my book. In the end, I chucked the book in the bin and muddled through. Silvano spent a lot of time with her and brought her everywhere he went. Everyone was so happy for me; there was great celebration at her birth. Nino and Nan Morelli were her godparents.

Two days before her christening, my father's brother, Angelo died. My dad came for both events, and it was the last time he came to Dublin. He didn't like moving from his own home and rarely went out, except to go to the bookies in the morning – his one vice was to have a little bet on the horses. He would try to sneak his way there as my mother would give him a hard time if she discovered where he had gone. He would pass his time studying the form and often won a few pounds on a double or a treble bet. We would always try to cover up for him.

That same year, in February, Silvano's sister, Anna got married to Aldo Fusciardi, whom she had met at our wedding. She left Dublin and set up home in Farnham in England. Nine months later she gave birth to her first daughter, Marisa.

* * *

Silvano and his friends decided to run the yearly Italian dress dance, which they did very successfully for many years, before handing it over to Club Italiano. They also got into speedboat racing. The boats were small and made of fibre-glass, with an engine at the back. They formed the Roma Club and competed around Ireland. We kept our boat in the potato shed. He called it 'Gigi' after his daughter, Angie, and it was no easy task climbing over it every time we had to get a sack of potatoes. Ten-pin bowling had just opened in Stillorgan and, true to form, all the men got interested. It was very popular with the Italian community and the alley would stay open late to accommodate them so, after work, that's were you would find them. My father-in-law was very keen on the game and joined a team called the 'Magnificent Seven'. He won many trophies. It was a couple of years before I got a chance to play, as pregnancies got in the way.

Angie was ten months old when I conceived again. About seven months into the pregnancy the doctor told me I was having a multiple birth, that they were getting two heartbeats. Ultrasound hadn't been invented yet, so they sent me for an x-ray in my eighth month. Sure enough, it confirmed I was having twins. I remember I could hardly walk upright, so I found walking on all fours was more comfortable. The twins were born on the 30th October, 1965 – a boy and a girl. Sandra came first and, a few minutes later, Sandro. She was dark with black curly hair, and he was blonde. Both had dark eyes and both weighed 6lbs 10z. Angie wasn't impressed when I brought the twins home. She was only eighteen months old and didn't think much of the intruders, but her father came to the rescue and paid a lot of attention to her. We were living with Silvano's family at the time as my father-in-law wanted to retire, and so he sold the business in Fairview to us. They were to leave and go to a private house but there was a delay in their moving, so it was a very difficult time for all of us. They still had two school-going children, Luisa and Roberto, in the house, and I had just one bedroom for three little ones, Silvano and myself. With two babies on three-hour feeds, and one toddler teething, the nights were a bit of a nightmare, with me trying my best to not have them crying too long, or all the others would be woken up too. The situation got unbearable so I lost it, called my brother to come and get me, and went home for ten weeks, until the others had moved out.

I really relished the time I had at home. Peggy came every day to help with the babies and I had a very relaxed time. Rina, my sister, was always ready to take Angie out for walks in her pram. I saw all my old friends and walked the country lanes of my youth. In Dublin, no one walked anywhere. They would even get the bus to go one or two stops distance. While at home, I discovered my sister Rina had a secret. She was seeing a local boy, Norman Best. He was a Protestant, and she had been seeing him for a long time. She was better than me at sneaking, and so far my mother hadn't found out about him. His mother knew about it but had no objection to my sister, so she would go to his house, leave Angie with her, and go off with Norman. I covered up for her while I was there, but I tried to warn her about what was in store if Mammy ever found out. Rina was working in a hairdressing salon, learning the trade, so that helped to cover up her movements to some extent. Eventually, though, she was caught, and once again war broke out in Café Rex. Rina, quiet but extremely stubborn, wouldn't fight when Mammy started on her, but would turn on her heel and walk away. This went on for many months, so Norman emigrated to Canada, believing the whole situation was impossible. He also wanted to find a better future for himself, but still corresponded with Rina every week, via the hairdressers. My father at this stage had stopped driving, so Mammy bought Rina a car, which she learned to drive fairly quickly. She would bring Mammy to Belfast to see her friend, or out and about, wherever she wanted to go; or she would drive to Dublin to visit me for a week or two. She, however, was caught receiving letters, and the saga began again. I remember one Christmas he sent her a beautiful Canadian jacket, but she didn't dare wear it, so she gave it to me. I enjoyed that jacket. Mario and I tried our best to reason with Mammy, but to no avail. She wasn't having it under any circumstances until, one morning, Rina drove her to Belfast with the understanding that someone else would be bringing her back home.

During the journey they were arguing about Norman. On the way back, after dropping her off, Rina had a bad accident on the motorway. Her front tyre burst and the car went into a wobble and hit the embankment and upended. She was taken to Lisburn hospital, unconscious, with head injuries and broken ribs. Rina was always putting hair pieces on her head, which were the fashion then. Hers was too big, so to make it fit, she had stuffed it with tights and cotton wool. This saved her from serious head trauma. It was several days before we knew the extent of the damage but, thank God, she recovered.

This brought about a change of heart, and my mother gave Rina permission for the relationship to go ahead. I was there when Norman called the house. His mother had told him about the accident and, for the first time in four years, they were able to talk on the phone without hiding. He flew home to see her, and they got engaged before he went back. They set their wedding for April, 1970.

Chapter Seven
- Changes -

1970 started off on a high note. My youngest sibling, Rina, was getting married in April and, for weeks, the preparations were full speed ahead. Indeed, we would sometimes get fed up with all the wedding talk and so, as a nice diversion, we all decided to go to the annual Irish-Italian dress dance which was held in February. This was our biggest social event, where we caught up with family and friends whom we hadn't seen in a while. Fathers, mothers and children from age fourteen were allowed to attend so, all in all, it was highly popular. In the Seventies, the music was mainly the big bands, and we were lucky that our friend Tom Cafolla was friendly with the Miami Show Band (lead singer Dickie Rock), so the dance was always a huge success and drew a large young Irish crowd as well. Those were the mad days of rock-and-roll and the wonderful 'jive' that burned off all the stresses and strains of life; the girls with their many coloured swirling skirts and stiletto heels, and the boys with their D.A. haircuts and drainpipe trousers.

* * *

We always knew when Angela was pregnant because she wouldn't talk to Mario. This caused great mirth in the family, as Mammy – as all mothers do – would try and defend my brother by announcing that it takes two to tango. Poor Angela, she loved the babies but hated the pregnancies as she was always very sick. She went on to have another girl and she named her Anita. This little girl came into the world one week before my sister's wedding. The only time my father ever tried to offer a name was for this baby; he said to call her Silvia. We are still laughing about this, wondering why and where he came up with Silvia.

The preparations for Rina's wedding kept me busy, as she hated trying on dresses and wasn't much interested in shopping. Her famous expression was "Couldn't be bothered." So, I took it upon myself to look for a wedding dress for her. I knew her likes and dislikes, as I had – most of the times she went to the dress dance – organised her outfit. We went to Arnott's in Dublin and chose a design, plus two bridesmaid's outfits. These lucky girls were Uncle Nick's daughters whom we had rarely seen, as they lived in London. Rina wanted her best friend Beatrice, but Mammy insisted. So, guess who won?

April of that year was also the start of change in the family's dynamics. Rina's wedding day arrived to brilliant sunshine and we were all in a jolly mood. The wedding went over nicely, and we all had a lovely day. I don't think, in the hustle and bustle of the day, anyone noticed my dad was feeling ill; or maybe, as is his usual character, he kept it hidden. Next day, he was pretty ill and was on oxygen for his lungs. A week later, Rina left Ireland and went to Canada to start her new life. My mother must have been broken hearted, as Rina was her baby, eight years younger than me, and the two of them were very close. Rina had always been there at home, while Mario and I had left to get married. Indeed now, with my own girls so many years in the States, I can really relate to my mother and her feelings; or perhaps, when one reaches old age, things become more clear and one's understanding sharpens.

My father seemed to rally around a few days later, so I returned to Dublin with my brood. Eight weeks later, Silvano and I were going to Portstewart to be godparents for Nicole Morelli, Nino and Nan's daughter, and stopped off at home to see my parents before we continued on our way. My father was ill, and Mammy was worried, so I told her I would return immediately after the christening. That evening, when I got back, he was much worse, so I decided to stay and Silvano went on to Dublin to look after the kids. Dad was taken to hospital and, two weeks later, he died. It was June, 1970. The day before he died he had a sudden surge of strength and he sat up in the bed and proceeded to talk about Pope Giovanni (John) XXIII. He told me he had been talking to him and that the reason he had to leave was to prepare a place for his family. He also told me not to think he had lost his marbles, that he knew who he was and what he was saying. When I saw him so well I assumed, wrongly, he was on the mend so I took the opportunity to go back to Dublin to check on my kids who were staying with their paternal grandparents. I had just reached home when the news came through that he had died. We were devastated. To my shame, I couldn't face seeing him dead so I stalled going back until he was in the coffin. An awful sense of loss surrounded me and still does to this day. Rina had just emigrated to Canada and didn't make it for the funeral so my mother, in a sense, lost both of them at the same time. Silvano brought the kids and I stayed with Mammy as long as I could. Café Rex would never be the same again.

* * *

At this same time, trouble was brewing in the North. Catholics were protesting against the system of government and were seeking 'one man, one vote' as, prior to this, only the head of the household had a vote. During a peaceful protest in Derry, the soldiers opened fire on the crowd. It was a terrible massacre. After that, things changed drastically. The year before my father's death, Mario had done a big renovation in the shop and flat, and when the troubles escalated, the business suffered a lot, as it was impossible to carry on in a normal fashion. Bombs were set off indiscriminately, and people's lives and livelihoods were destroyed. There were constant interruptions during the course of the day, and bomb scares were often the cause of people running out without having paid for their food. The British army moved in, and walls were built across the main street, at either end of the town, manned by armed soldiers, to stop traffic having access to the centre for fear of car bombs. There was, once again, mass emigration. People were searched before entering shops or banks, and it became too dangerous for my mother to stay in the flat above the shop, the home in which she had started her married life and had reared all her family; as it had been broken into, and all the religious artifacts damaged. She moved into the house with Mario, and the home where I was born and spent most of my life in, was never lived in again.

* * *

Rina and Norman had moved to Barrie, a town two hours from Toronto, where he was given a store to manage. For a time Rina worked in an off-licence, or 'liquor store' as they were called in Canada. She was never good at arithmetic, so when she had to estimate how many bottles of wine were needed for a certain amount of people, she would call Norman for help. She managed to keep the job as she used to shine the bottles on the shelves the way she had been taught at home with the mineral bottles, so they looked nice on the shelves. They were renting an apartment, and my mother decided to go and see how they were getting on. While she was there, she helped them to buy their first home, showing Norman how to go about it. She stayed four weeks and had a nice time helping Rina get organised. A year later, in February, Rina gave birth to her first daughter, Lisa. She brought her back to Ireland when she was a year old – a lovely child with blonde curls. All the family were mad about her, especially my mother. She was so happy to have them home for a while.

Chapter Eight
- Family Life -

Fairview was fairly central, about a fifteen minute walk from the city centre. The café was big, as was the adjoining house; it was an old Georgian building. The house had four bedrooms, two living rooms and a large kitchen. It was very spacious, and the rooms had high ceilings. The shop part had been built in what was originally the front garden. Directly opposite was a fairly big park, with a football pitch and a playground. My kids spent many happy hours in that park. The yard held two outhouses and a large garage. The kids were happy there, as they knew the other shopkeepers very well and would drop in and out for a chat.

Angela was a happy wee girl, loved playing house and dolls. She was a chatter box, and very affectionate. Her grandmother called her 'Bacia padocchia,' as she was always kissing us. She was very creative and was always painting or sewing or making something. She also loved sports – swimming, especially. She was like a fish in the water, and went on to be a competitive swimmer for which she won many medals. She would get so excited at Christmas and occasions that she would get a temperature. She loved travelling and going out and about. Sandra was a bundle of dynamite, always suspicious of people, but mad about animals. She cost me a fortune bringing stray, hurt animals to the vet. She loved football, and managed to get on to her brother's team, disguised as a boy. She called herself Philip and was great at the game. Eventually, the others found out she was a girl but she played so well that they kept her secret. Dolls were not on her list, and she managed to persuade us to get her a dog. She called him Trampus, and when anybody annoyed her she would set the dog on them. She also had a cat, a bird, a rabbit, and white mice which, thank God, I never saw; and goldfish.

Her twin, Sandro, was placid and, no matter what toy he got, he would take it apart and try to put it back together again, with emphasis on the word 'try'. His favourite pastimes were playing with LEGO and building Airfix models, which he spent hours doing. Every Christmas and birthday he would ask for these models. He hated walking, and sports of any kind, and was always first out of the pool when their dad took them swimming. Most of the time he played quietly by himself, lost in some dream world, never knowing what was going on in the family, but he was very creative.

The three of them were very close, and often Angela and Sandro would gang up against Sandra when she would tease them to death or try to blackmail them into doing something she wanted. Sandra and Mammy got on well together and she would often go and stay with her up North.

The business was opened from 11am to 1am, and Fridays were the busiest days, as families kept the fast then, and fish and chips were popular to bring home. Saturday nights were the most dreaded work nights, as there was – without fail – trouble of some sort. Fights broke out, and we often had to go and try to break them up. It was always nerve-wracking and we often worked under stress. Nearly every Italian lad would sport a black eye on Sunday morning. We had a big circle of friends from the old country, who were always dropping in. As a result, my mother always had company of her own age group when she stayed with us. She would visit Rita and John very often, and enjoyed her time in Dublin.

* * *

On 2nd July, 1971, I gave birth to my youngest son, almost a year to the day after my father's death. He brought me great comfort. We named him Silvano Rocco. He came into the world rather quickly, in the breech position, on a Friday lunchtime. He was a beautiful, blonde curly-haired baby, and his two sisters had a great time with their new baby brother. There was never any problem them babysitting him. He weighed 7lbs 5ozs and was a very smart little boy. When he started school at age four, the teacher told me he had a reading age of twelve. He picked things up very quickly, could spell difficult words, and the three older ones were always asking him how to spell words they were having trouble with. He was a placid little boy, but very stubborn; and forever asking questions. A friend of mine once brought him home in the car and, by the time he got to the house, he was all flustered from the barrage of questions, wondering how he was supposed to answer why a red light was red for stop and a green one was green for go. Silvano had to have his tonsils out when he was two, and because it was his father that had taken him into hospital, he wouldn't look at his dad when he was brought home from there. It took my husband quite a while to make friends with him again. He loved to get out in the car, and every time his father put his jacket on to go out, the little fellow would be ahead of him at the front door. Sometimes, my husband would rise from his chair and our little son would be up too, hoping to go with him – only to be disappointed by his father announcing, with some exasperation, that he was only going to the toilet. Sunday afternoons, they would all go to the Phoenix Park with their father to meet up with other Italian children. The men would play boccia, an Italian game something like bowls.

The year before Silvano junior's birth, I had employed a woman to help me with the housework. Her name was Liz and she had been recently widowed. She was from Tullow, near Carlow, and her doctor had advised her to go and stay with her sister in Dublin, to help with her depression after her husband's death. She and her sister weren't getting on, so she came to tell me she had to leave, explaining the situation. Instead, I took her in as a live-in help, and it was the best move I ever made. She helped with the children, especially Silvano jnr, and they became very close. She would take him to St. Stephens Green to feed the ducks, and to the zoo in the Phoenix Park. Liz would stay with us for twelve years. She was a great lady, and only died in 2005 at the ripe old age of ninety-seven. My son was there at her side as she slipped away, and we both attended her funeral with members of her family from England. We spent a lovely evening reminiscing and catching up. Silvano is truly a part of their family and always will be.

Chapter Nine
- More Changes -

We were considering buying a house for the children and moving Mammy to Dublin. Our plan was for her and Liz to mind the kids while we commuted to work, and also because it would be better for Mammy to live in Dublin. She was happy there and had plenty of visitors and people to visit, so we started to look into it. But alas, due to cruel circumstances, it wasn't to be.

The following year, my mother decided to go to Italy with my brother's family, to get out of the North for the month of July which was always a troublesome time up there. I was happy she was going to spend some nice sunny days with her sister and aunts. I left her to the airport and told her to stop with me on the way back for a few months. But, three weeks later, she called me saying she was feeling ill and asked could she come back. I asked her if she was able to travel alone, or did she want me to come and get her, but she assured me she could make the journey. I arranged for her to fly to Dublin and stay with me to recover. Silvano went to collect her. The plane was delayed for hours, and when she walked through the door of the house, I took one look at her and somehow knew that whatever she had, it couldn't be good; she was so thin, in just three weeks. I put her to bed and didn't sleep all night; I couldn't wait to call the doctor. Next morning, he came at 9am, and that was the beginning of a nightmare for me, as he told me he suspected a tumour. Before she left for Italy she had been through lots of tests in Belfast and had been given the all-clear. That evening, she was in hospital. My lovely mother was diagnosed with ovarian cancer (the 'silent killer', they called it). It was terminal and she was given two months to live. I can't put into words the emotions of that time, the pain of knowing that after her operation there was nothing they could do, and that she had eight weeks to live. The day I received this news, I can honestly say, I went into some kind of shock and didn't emerge for ten years. Still today, I feel the pain of that time of waiting and waiting for the end that I knew was inevitable. I decided against the doctors telling my mother that she was going to die, so they agreed but warned me they would inform her if she asked them directly. Rina was pregnant with her second child and made the journey home to spend time with Mammy. It was so hard putting up a front, and not breaking down. Mario would drive down and we tried to make this last time together special. Rina was heartbroken when she had to leave, knowing she would never see her again. Her last goodbye nearly broke all of us up with grief.

Every three months, Mammy had to go for chemotherapy and this involved a stay in hospital. It had very severe side-effects and she would be violently sick for days after, but it prolonged her life by a year and two months, long enough to know Rina's son David was born, and that Rina was safely over the caesarean birth. She knew by now that she wasn't going to live, and it seems she fought hard to stay until the baby was born, and then she let go. Mammy died the following week, on 15th September, 1974, four years after my father. It was also the feast of her village in Italy, and they had great celebrations there that day. A few hours before she died, she came out of a coma and stood on the floor, saying that my dad and her dad had come for her. As with my father, there was a great surge of energy in the room – I could feel it. Although I had feared this day for a long time – I thought I would let her down and run away, I was so afraid – at that time I seem to have received some kind of grace, and the fear left me. I was able to stay with her as she took her last breath. We brought her home to Portadown and laid her to rest beside my father in Drumcree. The journey back was tough as they were shooting in Newry and we were held up for a time.

At the same time, Rita's eldest son, Anthony, was very ill. He was in the same hospital as Mammy and they often visited each other. He was twenty-four years old and was to be married in September, but had a problem with his intestines. They operated, but it wasn't successful. He died the week before Mammy; they went home to God together. Rita never recovered from the death of her son, but would always say to me that at least he is with his Aunty Lidia. The days ahead were very bleak and I couldn't get the image of her year of suffering out of my head, no matter how hard I tried to picture the healthy woman, full of energy and life. It must have been so much more bleak for Rina, who was miles away from family and friends, and because of the section was unable to make the journey home. But we had children to see to, and this helped to keep us both going in those black days.

* * *

My in-laws decided to retire back to Italy, so we bought their house in Clontarf and moved in. The kids were delighted. They had a back garden with a tree to climb on, and already had friends in that area. Antoinette lived around the corner and her two girls and mine attended the same school. We had many friends and there was always some occasion to get together. The girls attended Holy Faith Convent, which was at the end of the road, while Sandro had to get a bus to O'Connell's, near the city centre. Silvano jnr's school was Belgrove, also near the house. He had friends on the road and they all settled quickly. The swimming pool was just up the road, so they were all busy. Sandro joined the scouts and he loved it so much he stayed till he was fifteen. He also played guitar, although he wanted an accordion. I convinced him to try guitar instead, which he learned very well. With a few friends, he started a little group and played in various gigs. The practice sessions were awful as they would play the same song over and over; it still rings in my head (*'My Best Friend's Girl'* - Arrgh!)

In the summer holidays, the kids would go to San Andrea to stay with their grandparents. Alfonso loved nothing better than having his grandchildren around him. He was a very outgoing, sociable man with a hearty laugh, and had many friends. Silvano and I stayed behind, as we had to pay off what we owed for the business, so it was seven years before we went back to Italy together. Silvano had a skin problem that occasionally brought him to hospital, so we decided to look for someone to help me in the shop. Robert brought a friend of his, Rosario, a young Italian from Naples, who was seeking work. We bought a fast-food in Harmonstown. It was near the house and easier for me to run, leaving Rosario and his family to look after the Fairview Grill. That summer, we had the chance to go to Italy all together as a family. We decided to go by car, and show the kids as many countries as we could. It was a great holiday as Anna and her family decided to go at the same time, so there was plenty of company for the kids, and they had a great time together. Anna's two girls, Marisa and Renata, would come over often to Ireland, and the cousins had great times together. In June of 1979, I decided to go and see my sister in Canada and brought all five teeny-boppers, plus a seven-year-old with me. We stayed for three weeks. It was nerve-wracking, but they had fun. I think my sister is still getting over the shock.

Chapter Ten

- Moving to Kerry -

Silvano's sister Luisa and her husband were selling their business in Killarney, with the intention of moving to Spain. We considered this move for over a year, as it was a big decision for us. Although it was a good financial move, we were torn with the idea of leaving family and friends, and the life we had known. It was particular harder on the younger ones, especially Angela, who was in her final year at school. I only realised later how difficult it was for them – change of schools and friends they had known all their lives. In the end, we decided to go, along with Rosario and family as partners. It was very hard to adjust to life in the country after the hustle and bustle of the city, not to mention trying to get used to the Kerry accent. I didn't understand them and they didn't understand my Northern accent, and we were all speaking English.

Seems like yesterday when Silvano and I embarked on the great adult world of marriage, prepared for the whole mission with no education, no schooling in business whatsoever. Handed a bunch of keys and thrown out with the bath water, to open and run our first chipper in Glasnevin. We got our own brood of four kiddos, headed for the hills, bag and baggage, and hoofed it down to Killarney.

We rented a house initially, and the only house available at the time was a mile and a half out of town. Although it was a lovely bungalow in a beautiful setting, I couldn't get used to the quiet, and was depressed a lot of the time. Nature was all around us. Cows would wander into the garden. One time, I even found a donkey in our shed. Angie had agreed to come with us for a year, and if she didn't like it or couldn't settle she would return to Dublin.

The kids headed off for their various schools, while we adults reported for duty to run the Allegro self-service in High Street. It was a very modern self-service, way ahead of its time. Staff would bring other family members to start work there too, and it made for a lovely atmosphere.

The business was very different from what we were used to. It was a very big self-service, seated a lot of people, and the summers were hectic, with American and European tourists flocking in. The twins took to the place very fast, but Angie and I were struggling. Liz decided to go home to Tullow, and didn't make the move with us. But she didn't retire. At the age of seventy-five, she started another job and stayed in it for ten more years.

Eleven-year-old Silvano jnr. had decided he was 'Cato' from the Inspector Clouseau films, and loved jumping out at people. The self-service became his favourite hunting ground. One incident lives long in the memory. We had employed an Italian to head up our take-away, a nice unassuming man called Antonio. One day, Antonio saw a banana lying on the floor and, being a conscientious employee, bent down to pick it up and put it back in the press. As soon as he opened the door, Silvano, with arms flailing, jumped out and screamed at him. My scheming son had placed the banana on the floor and had spent over an hour lying on a shelf in the press, hoping someone would pick it up. How Antonio wasn't taken to hospital that day I don't know. Years later, Silvano says he can still see his face. Sorry, Antonio!

While Silvano (whose name was squashed to Bam, thanks to his love of Pebbles and Bamm Bamm) got up to mischief in the restaurant, I was always worried and forever trying to keep track of the twins – they were always up to something. In the city I always knew where they were, but Killarney was a different story. It may have been a smaller town, but I guess it was still easier not to be found. There were not many fellow Italians there to report back to me. When the twins left school, the two girls decided to go inter-railing around Europe, for eight weeks. I never did get the whole story on that trip, and maybe it's just as well.

After a while, Angie had enough and returned to Dublin. For a while she worked in the Fairview Grill, while she studied for a beautician course. At the same time, Sandra decided to try her hand at hairdressing. Fairview was becoming difficult to keep and we decided to sell it, so they both stayed with their father's brother, Adriano, until they qualified. In the meantime, Sandro had spent some three months in Italy helping his grandparents, as my father-in-law was ill and couldn't drive. During his stay, he met Paola, a young girl from Rome who was visiting her grandmother who lived in Casalattico. They fell in love and, after a year, got engaged. Paola worked for Air India and had free travel so she came to Killarney quite often.

On 14th March, 1985, Silvano's father died after a long illness. After the funeral, Angelina left Italy and settled in Spain for a year with her daughters. It was a very difficult time for her, and she couldn't settle there, so she returned to Ireland and spent some months with us in Killarney, and some months in Dublin. We would take her to Italy every year for a couple of months, but she was very disoriented and couldn't seem to find her niche. She had been so dependent on her husband that she found making decisions impossible, but that was the way for women of her era, and change was too difficult. Perhaps, had she been a younger woman, it might have been easier to make a new life.

On 14th December that same year, Sandro and Paola got married in Rome. Angela and Sandra were in the middle of their final exams, but managed to fly over for a weekend to attend the wedding. The following year, my first grandchild was born. They named her Sara.

Angela qualified as an aesthetician and, with her friend, moved to London, where she started work in a health studio in Knightsbridge. After several months she got bored with this type of work, so she did an intensive course in word-processing over a weekend, and started a new office job. She stayed in London for two years, then returned to Dublin and worked for an accountant in St. Stephen's Green. Sometime later, she entered the green card lottery for America, which she was lucky to get, and set off for Cape Cod to open it up. From there, she went to Boston, where she worked in a youth hostel. She made many good friends there. She decided to enter her sister's name in the lottery for a green card, and she too was successful, so Sandra went off to Detroit to try her luck in America. She wasn't too happy there so when her friend Linda, who was in the Cayman Islands, sent for her, she settled on the island for three years, met a young man, and brought him home to Ireland to meet us. They stayed for a year and helped to organise a new business Robert and Sandro had opened, but they later decided to return to the Cayman Islands. After this, they went to Florida and, for a year, lived in Clearwater.

While they were there, my sister-in-law Angela and myself decided to go and visit them. Angie and her boyfriend Steve were driving down from Boston to meet us as well as my sister Rina, who was making the journey from Toronto. We stayed with them for a few days, and then Sandra's fella got us a house in a place across the road from them, called Parsley Park. It was a fine big house with a dock outside. The only problem was, it was a senior citizen's area, and it had more rules than the army! The elderly people rode around the street on three-wheeler bicycles. It was not what we had in mind for a yahoo time in Florida – I never saw this place on the holiday brochures. We had the greatest laugh ever in that place. To make it up, we would stroll up the beach to the Hilton hotel and have pina coladas. Florida was great. We went to all the theme parks, and had a great time. Sandra was under a bit of a strain, as she wasn't getting on too well with her man. After we left they went back to the Cayman Islands, where Sandra broke it off and came home to Ireland for a few months.

Silvano jnr. had finished school and had started working in the self-service. He was extremely good on the cash, as he was very fast adding up the trays, but after a couple of years of this he got bored and decided to go back and try for his leaving certificate again, which he studied for in a one-year intensive course in Cork. He had admittedly been lazy on his first attempt but did well this time and was accepted into Trinity College in Dublin, to study Occupational Therapy. This unfortunately ended up not really suiting him so he came back to the restaurant. Years later, he would obtain a degree in Catholic theology, and enjoys writing about faith and life.

My husband's youngest brother, Robert, had just completed a bungalow for his family and was living in it for seven months when his marriage broke up, so we bought it from him and moved into Ross Road. It had a very large garden, and Silvano spent many enjoyable hours in it. Silvano jnr. also enjoyed the new house. He, like his brother before him, with four friends formed a group and, like his brother, played guitar. They called themselves 'Congress 27', Silvano played the bass, and even if I say so myself, they were very good and played in a lot of places, but unfortunately there were a lot of arguments among themselves so they broke up. Another time later, he joined up with a few others and played the music of my rock-and-roll days, so when they used my garage for practice I would be dancing around the kitchen, thoroughly enjoying myself singing to the music. This too ran its course.

Sandro and Paola had their second child, a boy they named Stefano. Two days later, the world's stock markets crashed. Had they heard that Stefano had been born? They had a house down the road from us, and the two children spent a lot of time with us. Paola spoke Italian to them all the time, so in looking after the children my Italian improved immensely. We took them on a lot of walks, into the forest, and to all the local nature trails. Every summer they spent with their maternal grandparents in Rome.

* * *

The next few years were rough for my brother. The troubles were intensifying in the North, and the situation was dangerous, as one never knew where or when the next bomb would go off. It affected business badly, and eventually the Café Rex was forced to close, and was later sold. For me, it was the end of an era, and I felt sad thinking about it. Although it was only a building, we had all been born there, it held all the memories of my youth, and we had laughed, played and cried, loved and argued, all within its walls. Another fast-food shop that Mario had opened in the same town was petrol bombed. With no income, he was forced to move. Together with Silvano and others they opened a business in Clonmel, and settled there for two years. They managed, with the help of their son Riccardo, to get a small house and they moved what was left of their furniture and belongings into it, and set up home. Their son Italo joined them, and Anita the youngest daughter, but circumstances forced them to pack up and move again. Their eldest son got married and needed the house, so it was decided they would come to live and work with us in Killarney. I was very worried about them, as the thought of moving bag and baggage again had both of them very depressed. So, I packed up all their stuff and helped them make the move. They would work the summer season, then go to Italy for the winter months to look after Angelina's father, who had retired there and was in his eighties. But they were unsettled, still had no home of their own and their family were scattered. Angela was very often depressed about her situation. Cooking was her forte, so she settled into working in the kitchen of our restaurant, the 'Allegro', and soon made friends with her workmates, in particular a woman called Mary O Donoghue.

One day, Mary invited her to a prayer meeting she was active in with her husband, Geoff. When she returned that evening, there was something different about her. She looked glowing, and began to share her experience with us. Mario, being very skeptical, sent me with her the following day to suss it out as he thought his wife was very gullible, and was afraid she had joined some sect or other. I went along and can honestly say it was the beginning of tremendous change in my life. It was a charismatic meeting, very different from what I was used to. People were singing, and some were sharing their stories. At the end, prayer lines were formed, and one by one we had personal prayer.

I remember a great feeling of elation, and at the same time I couldn't get my head around the experience. All my life I had been an ardent reader, loved a good book in preference to watching television, but had never read the Bible, so first thing I did was buy a Bible. I must have received a special time of grace, because for the next two years I couldn't leave it down; I read nothing else. Through these meetings I made the best, most genuine friends ever. When trouble hit, we would get together and pray for each one's situation, without needing to know the details. It became a way of life for Angela and I. This was August, 1988. Our husbands at the time were concerned. I suppose they thought we were becoming fanatical. It's funny, but had we been out every night drinking or whooping it up, or doing the so called 'normal' things, it wouldn't have had such an effect, but for us it was the beginning of a walk that changed us forever. All the depressions of the past seemed to be healed as we discovered the power of prayer in our lives and the joy it brought to our lives – a special time of learning and getting to know the Jesus of the Bible, and the wonderful friends we made then and since. These were lovely years we spent together. A few years later, Angelina's father died and left her a business in Newry, Co. Down. She and Mario moved back North, and settled there. Slowly, her children followed, married and settled around them. The Lord restored to them what they had lost. They became the proud grandparents of fourteen children.

Angela passed away in October of 2014, and my dear brother Mario followed her almost two years later, on the 15th of August, 2016, the feast day of the Assumption of the Blessed Virgin Mary. Both were surrounded by their family in the days leading up to their passing. I miss them both very much, especially my dear brother, who was such a strong and loving presence in my life for so long.

Chapter Eleven

- Life Goes On -

Angela met a young man from Wisconsin while she was working in a youth hostel in Boston – the aforementioned Steve – and took him home to meet us. He was an art student, very tall and slim, with long curly hair, and sported an earring. He wore some crazy looking hats, and big boots laced up the front. In other words, he stood out in a crowd. But we liked him a lot, and had lots of laughs at his antics. Silvano jnr. – who met him on a trip to visit his sister in Boston – liked him immediately, especially when he saw he had similar taste in music. Looking back, we must have scared him a bit, as we were a bit different from his own family, who were very polite people and only said nice things to each other. We, on the other hand, were rather blunt, and said what we thought; good, bad or indifferent. But he loved our expressions and adopted many of our sayings, which he thought were hilarious. He stayed for three months.

To earn some money, Angie and he painted Robert's Pizzeria, then took off for Rome where a friend of his was living for a summer. He made food-money by painting t-shirts, which he sold in the railway station and in the underground metro, running for his life every time he spotted a policeman. He learned that 'pizza bianca', or white pizza, was the cheapest food he could buy, so he lived on that for a few months until we got to Italy. Then he joined us in San Andrea for a few weeks and painted some rooms for us, to earn the money to go with Angie to Venice and Florence, before he returned to America. A few weeks later, Angie joined him in Wisconsin and shared an apartment with a friend of his, also called Angie, in Milwaukee. They stayed there for a year but didn't like it, and so returned to Boston. They set up home in Jamaica Plain, and she got a great job, in a health insurance centre. Steve was at this stage up to all kinds of jobs, from selling furniture to renovating houses; putting siding on walls to making frames for an artist teacher of his; anything and everything to make the rent money while he finished his studies in the museum of fine arts.

In September of 1994, Angie came home with an engagement ring, and we planned the wedding for the following June 26th. It was a bit difficult to arrange a wedding with her living in America, and it caused many arguments as she would dig her heels in on many issues. She chose a very old manor house in Kenmare for her reception – the wedding suite being in a tree-house caught her attention – but the hotel only catered for 115, and this for me caused some problems as I had to cut down a lot on the guest list; but I soldiered on. It was her day, and I conceded. Angie and Steve's wedding was unforgettable! It was a beautiful day, the sun blazed down, and everyone still talks about the great time they had. They were married in the cathedral in Killarney, with the help of a very special priest friend of ours, and the scenic journey to Kenmare over the mountains was beautiful. After the dinner, many people changed into casual clothes and enjoyed the beautiful gardens and sunshine. Debora, my niece who lives in Spain, danced flamenco, and a few children gave a demonstration of Irish dancing which the American guests thoroughly enjoyed. A friend of ours, Peter Salveta, had arrived from Dublin in a little bubble of a car, which a few of the lads had great fun in lifting up out of the car park and carrying down the garden to hide it behind a bush.

We also had the added entertainment of the 'exploding chairs.' The hotel had set out cheap plastic garden chairs, and every now and then, during dinner or the speeches, there would be a huge crash and all heads would turn and see some poor guest looking up bewildered from floor level, after having leaned back on the hind legs. The hotel were mortified, but we all had a good laugh over it. The weather was beautiful, we had a whole hotel and grounds to ourselves, and the sea was just metres away. It was one of the great days – even if the chairs kept exploding.

My eldest son, Sandro, in his own strange way, has managed to stay married after thirty-odd years now. We joke that his wife has had the patience of a saint. His pet phrase when asked anything is 'Leave me alone!' I say this in good humour – a sense of humour I know he shares. We always had a good relationship, Sandro and I. Maybe it takes one to know one, and may I say for him, he got the perfect wife, and they have, by the grace of God, put in a lot of years together and, please God, many more to come.

Then there's our Sandra, a free spirit whose generous, loving nature has brought her to a place she loves where she can grow and flourish and be of some good as she has always wanted. The remainder of her tale is yet to be told and I am sure that, one day, she will tell it herself.

The Lord has also blessed me with wonderful grandchildren. The eldest, Sara, is now in London working behind the scenes in the movies. She met and married Tom, a lovely young man working in the same field as her. The second, Stefano, has spent many years in seminary and seems set on becoming a priest, if and when the right time comes. He has a great love for God and for people, and I am sure the Lord will be his guide.

Sabina is my third grandchild, Sandro and Paola's second daughter. She was born in July, 1997, and brightens our lives with her wonderful character. Clay, my American grandson, was born to Angie and Steve in September of the same year and spent many summers with us, becoming great friends with Sabina at the same time. He is now striving to find his niche in the world too. We had to wait a full fourteen years before Silvano jnr. and his wife Viera gave us our fifth grandchild in May, 2011. She is the love of our lives, the beautiful and gentle Chiara, who never ceases to bring out the best in us and fills our days with so much love that it hurts. As my son, her father, so beautifully put it, she carries the tender cross of Down syndrome, and had to undergo open heart surgery at just five months of age, which was, thankfully, a great success. A sixth grandchild, Rocco, named after my loving father, came along four years later. He is like his father when he was a child, very smart and with a head of rolling blonde curls. Chiara and Rocco's mother is a gentle Slovakian girl that my son fell in love with after they met at a prayer meeting at a friend's house. They married in August, 2010 and are a very well-matched couple who live their lives united in their beliefs and faith. I know this will carry them forward through all of life's challenges that lie ahead. Whatever decisions they take, I am sure God will be the main advisor.

Angela, my first-born 'miracle baby' continues to regale my life with her highs and lows – certainly not a boring life. She is my butterfly, constantly flitting from place to place, job to job, and, with Steve, striving to make her way in a far-off land and raise her son to be a good man. He is flying the nest now, finding his wings, but, I would say, also keeping his heart close to home. Angela has at last settled into a fine corporate job, having fought with all her might against her hippy heart to do so. God is good.

* * *

All in all, Silvano and I have made tons of mistakes over the more than fifty years of our marriage, but we have always been united in our love and caring of both families, his and mine. He has been a good husband and father, has always looked after us well, and still does. I am sure I don't make his life a bed of roses as I am always telling him what he didn't do, but that's what wives do, I guess.

I have had a good life, always had love in my life – and laughter, good friends, and of course I have had my share of bad pain and grief, ups and downs; but in the midst of it all, I always had my friend, Jesus. He saw me through and still does. Without faith and God in your life, it has got to be hard.

I am writing this part of the book in my mother's village, where the story began. I can sense her there and, in my mind's eye, I can see the young Lidia enjoying the beautiful mountains that surround us; where she grew up, went to school, and mourned the loss of her mother, Marianna. I feel her in the little church where she was baptised and made her Communion and Confirmation. I feel her all around, especially here in Casalattico, and I feel close to her.

Life is a journey with many stops on the way. It's important to remember we are mere humans, we make bad mistakes and we must forgive ourselves and move on with the hard task in hand. It's always there ready, as are our hands always there to help our own offspring back up on their feet to stand tall again.

I salute my children, grandchildren, daughters-in-law, son-in-law, and my beloved husband. I thank them all for their love and respect in spite of my interfering tongue and nosey questions. I know it drives them mad, but then, isn't that my job?

*

Epilogue

- The End of the Beginning –

My dear mother Maria Taddei passed from this life on April 23rd, 2019, peacefully at home, with her husband Silvano by her side. She was 79. A great prayer warrior, she died on what, had it not been the Easter Octave, would have been St. George's Day, the slayer of the metaphorical dragon.

Her beloved daughter, and my sister, Sandra, passed away in October of 2018, after a three year battle with the same type of cancer that took Maria's mother all those years before. She was just 52. The day of Mum's funeral Mass was six months to the day that Sandra left us. It also would have normally been the Feast of Our Lady of Good Counsel. During Maria's life, as many could testify, there were many that received the gift of a listening ear, help, counsel and advice.

Sara and her husband Tom were blessed with a little girl, who was born in England on March 23rd, a month before Mum left us. Maria never got to meet little Gabriella, but she wanted her first great-grandchild to know that she loved her very much.

Mum's ashes arrived back to my father on May 1st, the day they would have celebrated their 57th

wedding anniversary. We had already planned to bring Sandra's ashes to Italy for interment in May of 2019, to Casalattico, where this story began. As it happened, both mother and daughter were laid to rest close to each other in that same beautiful place among the hills. It was May 18th, the same date that Mum had received her first Holy Communion, many years before, and the anniversary of the day the aforementioned battle for Montecassino ended.

Mum was one of a kind. She suffered much in her later years as her lungs slowly deteriorated from advanced COPD. If she could say something now, it would be to give up smoking as soon as you can. She would also say: Trust in God; Jesus loves you; Don't be afraid. It's the end of her story in this life, and what a story it has been. As with Montecassino, her battle, and that of my sister before her, is now over. But it's only the end of the beginning, for life goes on. Life is a journey. Maria's journey is over, but her destination is eternal. This life was only the beginning. I feel her presence still, I feel her help, and I hope and expect that she will continue to help us through life. For our Mammy, it could not really be any other way. Rest in peace, love and joy, Mum, thank you for everything, and we hope to see you and Sandra in Heaven someday.

> Your loving son,
> Silvano x

Printed in Great Britain
by Amazon